FORGIVENESS MADE EASY

The Revolutionary Guide to Moving Beyond Your Past
and Truly Letting Go

by Barbara J. Hunt

Cover Artwork: Jared P Meuser

Cover Design: Taylor Madison Damion

Author's photo: Jono Allin

Editor: C.D.

Copy Editor: Fiona Milligan

CONTENTS

To peace in every heart

all around the world

INTRODUCTION

*"Everyone thinks forgiveness is a lovely idea
until they have something to forgive."*

C.S.Lewis

"I'll never be able to forgive you for that."

Sarah is part of the way through her forgiveness process. She's sitting in her bedroom and the Skype connection seems to be affected by the strength of her feelings. Her image freezes momentarily.

I'm at my computer, thousands of miles away, facilitating an imaginary conversation between her and her father. She's got to the part where, in her imagination, she's telling him everything she's always wanted him to hear, right to his face. All of her anger and pain, detailing all of the consequences his behaviour had on their family and her life. At this point in the process she feels she can't ever forgive him.

This is her story:

"I don't have many memories of my father. The few I have are of my efforts to gain his love and attention. My father always had a reason to be anywhere other than at home helping my mother raise us six kids. When I was 8 years old, he found another woman. My mother was deeply hurt and they divorced when I was 14. I was very angry with my father because I felt he'd chosen someone else over us. I wanted nothing to do with him. After my mother moved us out of

state, I never returned to visit my father and he made few attempts to have a relationship with me. It would be another 20 years before I visited him again in our hometown.

The years following our separation from my father were a great struggle, and I wanted to blame him for all the pain. I so desired connection to a father figure that eventually a perpetrator filled that void. After years of grooming and brainwashing, my abuser gained so much power and influence over me and my two sisters that he was able to take us away from our family and friends for almost 15 years. He kept us separated from nearly everyone, in isolation, using fear to control us. Again, I wanted to blame my father. I believed that if he'd been there for us this man would never have been able to take us.

When I was 32, my abuser passed away and I was reunited with my family. In the years following I began to unravel my past and start the healing journey. It wasn't easy facing the pain, but it was the beginning of freedom. Healing from the emotional trauma and abuse I had endured for so much of my life took a lot of deep inner work.

I'd learned about forgiveness in my early years through religious teachings but I had a distorted view of what it meant. I thought it was the excusing of someone's behaviour. I believed that if I forgave someone I'd be letting them off the hook for what they'd done and then they would be free but I would still be imprisoned because of the hurt they had caused me. And, in some strange way, I felt that as long as I hung on to some anger they couldn't hurt me again. It was my protector.

After I started using the Forgiveness Made Easy process I began to realise that it was quite the opposite. Forgiveness was **my** freedom. Forgiveness was the key to unlocking **my** prison cell and setting **me** free. Yes, the other person received a benefit because my negative *energy and anger was no longer being projected at them. But, forgiveness set me free from living day in and day out with all of the* negative energy and anger that was destroying my body, mind, and *soul. Forgiveness was the only way I was going get out of my inner bondage.*

My first forgiveness session with Barbara was focused on my father. Saying everything I had always wanted to say to him but never could put into words before. At first the dialogue was intense and full of anger. But as the hidden emotions were released I began to feel light and free.

When the process was complete, I felt so much peace. I forgave my father for the past and set him free from the expectation of being the perfect father and I accepted him for who he is.

The big surprise was that after I started working with the forgiveness process, my father began reaching out to me more. We now speak more openly and transparently than ever before and our relationship is growing. I no longer carry the intense anger or disappointment I had towards him. I've let go of all expectations of what our relationship should be and I am allowing myself to enjoy it just as it is. I accept us both where we are on this journey of life. There are trigger moments of the past, but the intense emotion that used to come up with it isn't there anymore. I feel peace and acceptance in its place.

My divorced parents of 25 years have also become friends and my five siblings have begun to build new relationships with my father as well. I attribute our relationship transformation to the forgiveness process. A true miracle has occurred within our family! Every relationship I have worked through with this process has transformed in some way or another - and all for the better. I even did a forgiveness process on my abuser, which was another layer of deep healing.

I wouldn't be where I am today without using the forgiveness process. I feel more alive and free than ever before! The past is the past and the future is NOW."

Like Sarah, you might be thinking there is someone in your life you will never be able to forgive. Or, you might be willing to forgive but have no idea how to do it or where to start. I don't know anyone who hasn't struggled to forgive *someone*. The details of our stories might be different but what it takes to forgive is the same.

Forgiveness is a complex subject. It is profound, emotional, often misunderstood, full of unquestioned assumptions and mostly just avoided. The need to forgive someone can feel as uncomfortable and challenging as the prospect of giving up an addiction. Even the *thought* of forgiveness can evoke a high level of fear and resistance.

But most people don't know what forgiveness really is. They don't know why they can't let go of their hurt or resentment or realise how much suffering it's causing them. They also don't know how greatly they will benefit if they *do* forgive.

What is it about the idea of voluntarily letting go of our grievances that can make it seem like one of the hardest things we can ever do? There are many reasons why forgiveness seems so hard. There are subtle (and not so subtle) layers of resistance within us. If you want to effectively and authentically forgive, you need to understand what you're holding on to before you can let it go. In my work, I've found there are five main obstacles to forgiveness:

- **Misunderstanding** – what forgiveness is, and is not
- **Vulnerability** – all the fears that surround forgiveness

- **Ego** – the secret benefits of not forgiving
- **Resentment** – not knowing the hidden price you pay when you don't forgive
- **Know How** – having a forgiveness method that *works*

Forgiveness can also seem hard because you need to be willing to face your feelings about past hurts and the current challenges in your life. It can mean questioning some fundamental assumptions about life including your story about your past. It requires a depth of honesty, authenticity and self-compassion you might, at times, doubt that you can access.

However, with the perspectives and techniques offered in this book, the choice about whether or not to forgive is entirely in your hands. There's nothing external that has to change before you do it. You don't need to wait for the other person to make the first move, or apologise, or repent. Forgiveness is for *you* - not the other person. It's something you do inside yourself that you feel in your body and heart that releases you from your past and frees you to live life fully.

There's nothing you can do to change what happened in the past. But with forgiveness it can feel as if you have resolved the past, once and for all. You set yourself free from its power over you. Sometimes there will be beneficial changes in your relationships too, but the greatest benefit of forgiveness is a feeling of peace and lightness in your heart.

I wrote this book because I see forgiveness as a fundamental life skill that is rarely taught. Or, if it is, not taught at the necessary depth to be effective, let alone transformational. I want to help liberate forgiveness from the province of religious doctrines, clear up misunderstandings about what it is (and isn't) and make the practice of forgiveness relevant to our busy daily lives. I offer a forgiveness practice that is simple, effective, and easy.

I also want to champion its everyday use. In our increasingly connected world everything is about relationships, and forgiveness is essential for every kind of relationship we have. Forgiveness can transform our closest and most deeply intimate relationships as well as the casual, distant or formal ones.

If you're like most people, you take the bins out when they're full, and go to see the dentist for a check-up every now and then. You might not enjoy doing either of these things, but you do them nevertheless. Or maybe you'll exercise or meditate even when you don't really feel like it. Taking care of your emotional build-up is the same. Forgiveness is mental, emotional and spiritual hygiene, which, like gum disease, also happens to be related to your general wellbeing and the health of your heart.

Forgiveness is good for your physical health in other ways too. It reduces stress and lowers cortisol — the hormone linked to degenerative disease, lowered immune function and increased weight gain. There is mounting scientific evidence that it's one of the greatest things you can do for your health, wealth and creativity.

But forgiveness is like a superpower that hardly anyone ever uses - and that has intrigued me. Over the past 25 years as a mentor and coach, each one of my amazing clients has needed to do some forgiveness work on something, or someone, to help them move beyond their past. I've witnessed many of them struggle to forgive and have discovered the most common mistakes everyone makes. I've learned first-hand what works and what doesn't. I've also found ways to help overcome each obstacle to forgiveness and how to make the practice of forgiveness seem easy.

In the chapters that follow, I'll look at why forgiveness matters both for yourself and others and why it's so phenomenally good for you mentally, emotionally, physically and spiritually. I'll dive deeply into the reasons why, despite its many benefits, it seems so hard to do. I will also unravel the different kinds of resistance we have to forgiveness and how to address each one. As you go through the chapters of this book, you'll be able to see through, and overcome, each of the obstacles that may have been in your way. Forgiveness will seem more and more possible.

In chapter nine, I outline the seven-step Forgiveness Made Easy process, which is a simplified version of the one I guide my clients through. It's so straightforward you'll be able to do this process by yourself and experience all the benefits of forgiveness immediately.

You could also choose to buddy up and work through the steps with a friend. However, if you picked up this book because you know you need to forgive someone for significant trauma, I recommend that you seek professional help from a therapist, forgiveness coach or mentor who can support you with your process. (See the resources section at the back of the book for further details.)

I've also made suggestions for contemplation and journaling at the end of each chapter, so you can be preparing yourself to do your forgiveness work as you read through the book.

My intention is to help you look at forgiveness in such a way that you will naturally, honestly and authentically *want* to forgive whatever is unresolved in your heart. Forgiveness, once you know how to do it, is transformational. It will bring you a freedom and a peace that will make your whole life feel easier. Without it, there's just the slow internal encrustation of the heart over years and years that restricts the flow of connection and love.

I've helped hundreds of people go through the process of forgiveness and let go of their ill will and I've never had anyone ask to have their resentment back again!

As you begin this book I invite you to forget everything you think you already know about forgiveness. Whatever your experience with it has been so far in your life, here is your opportunity to meet forgiveness afresh and learn how to use it to change your life, and your world, for the better.

PART ONE
WHY IT MATTERS

"Without forgiveness, there really is no future."

Archbishop Desmond Tutu

CHAPTER ONE
WHAT IS FORGIVENESS?

"No gift of Heaven has been more misunderstood
than has forgiveness."

A Course in Miracles

The first obstacle to forgiveness is often a simple misunderstanding of what forgiveness is - and what it isn't. If you have a definition of forgiveness that truly reflects what forgiveness is, the rest of the process will be easier for you. I'm going to use K. Bradford Brown's definition:

> "Forgiveness is...
> the absolute refusal
> to hold ill will
> against someone (or something)
> for what they did
> or didn't do."

I love this because it puts the power wholly in your hands. Regardless of what someone has done or not done, the choice of whether or not to hold ill will is yours and yours alone. It's simple, but profound. It doesn't change whatever happened, because you can't change the past. But even when you have no power to influence an external situation, you do have the power to choose whether or not you will carry resentment about it afterwards.

The word that's translated as 'forgiveness' in the Bible is from the Greek 'aphesis' which means 'to let go'. But I want to make it clear that my approach to forgiveness is not based on any religion at all. You don't have to subscribe to a 'spiritual but not religious' worldview to do it, either. You simply have to be a human being who's in pain and wants that pain to stop.

Forgiveness is the straightforward action of absolutely refusing to hold ill will. That's it. You drop your resentment. You free yourself from your grievances. You undo the chains that have bound you to the past. Nelson Mandela knew this important truth.

"As I walked out the door toward the gate that would lead to my freedom, I knew that if I didn't leave my bitterness and hatred behind, I'd still be in prison." Mandela demonstrated that if you choose to let go of your ill will, grievances, anger and pain, you can forgive anything. He also showed us you don't have to march angrily for peace – you can just march. You can honour your values, maintain your boundaries, even put strong sanctions in place if necessary, without harbouring any ill will at all.

WHAT FORGIVENESS ISN'T

Letting go of ill will and resentment might sound simple, and it is, but it only starts to become *easy* once you know what's been getting in your way. In my approach to forgiveness, it's necessary to question and let go of all the inaccurate assumptions and misperceptions around what forgiveness is. The easiest way to do this is to look at what else forgiveness is *not.* Forgiveness is:

Not weakness
Not a feeling – you may never 'feel like' forgiving. You choose to
Not a way of avoiding painful feelings or the truth about the past
Not feeling OK about something – you might still feel anger and hatred about it

Not letting someone off the hook or letting people walk all over you
Not abandoning important values
Not saying something's OK with you when it's not
Not trivialising what happened
Not condoning, rationalising or excusing unacceptable behaviour

Not instead of, or the same as, restorative justice
Not forgetting or dishonouring the past
Not the same as cutting someone out of your life

Not a way of staying in unhealthy or abusive relationships or circumstances
Not reconciling old relationships
Not automatically trusting someone again

Not just for extreme circumstances
Not pointless because the past is over

Not something that will happen naturally if you wait long enough
Not dependent on the other person taking responsibility, apologising or making amends

That's quite a list. You can probably see where many of the difficulties we have with forgiveness begin. It's in the same place so many other difficulties in life begin - with misunderstanding.

Forgiveness doesn't stop you from speaking up or protesting when there's injustice. You can forgive but also keep clear boundaries, keep the law and vote with your feet if you are in danger. All of these things can be done without the poison of resentment flowing through your veins at the same time.

As Archbishop Desmond Tutu says; "Forgiveness is not opposed to justice, especially if it is not punitive justice, but restorative justice, justice that does not seek primarily to punish the perpetrator... but looks to heal a breach, to restore a social equilibrium that the atrocity or misdeed has disturbed."

MY STORY

I was raised as a Catholic, went to a Catholic girls' school and was taught all the stories from that tradition, about turning the other cheek and forgiving seventy times seven. But I didn't really think forgiveness applied to me. It seemed to be an unrealistic ideal achievable only by saints and martyrs and necessary only in extreme cases.

My early encounters with the idea of forgiveness were the usual childhood ones. Once, my sister tried to lose me when we were on holiday by telling me the wrong way back to the chalet. We were finally found, scolded and told to make up, "Say you're sorry to your sister!" We then had to parrot back an unenthusiastic and inauthentic "Sorry".

My sister seemed to hate me for existing (as older sisters sometimes do) and there were many occasions when she was mean and unkind to me, but I don't remember ever thinking I needed to forgive her for anything, or even that I was holding any resentment against her.

It wasn't until I was almost 30 that I had an epiphany about forgiveness. I was participating in a personal development workshop and it dawned on me that I had been holding resentment against my mother for years because of her illness. She had multiple sclerosis and by the time I was 15 years old it was having a significant impact on my whole family. I was in denial about my resentment and didn't know what to do with all my uncomfortable feelings because it wasn't anyone's fault.

This is another example of how hard it can be to recognise the need to forgive. If you'd asked me at the time if I resented my mother for being ill I would have honestly said, "No", because I wasn't aware of it. I was just coping with very challenging circumstances and trying to be nice about it.

Life goes on, enough water passes under the bridge, you grow up, you rationalise, sometimes you seem to forget and something similar to forgiveness seems to happen by itself. What I've observed, however, is that this appearance of reconciling the past is just like ice on top of a frozen puddle. The muddy water is still there underneath. You only need to put a tiny amount of pressure on the ice and it will crack. This is what happened with my resentment of my mother's illness. It was only decades later that I discovered the impact my resentment was having on my whole life.

Time doesn't necessarily heal all things. Some things wait to be forgiven. If you just try to overlook something significant it can be like trying to heal a wound while the knife is still in it. Every unresolved internal issue waits until you are ready to face it and feel it. Sometimes, especially when you're younger and something difficult happens, you don't have the emotional capacity to deal with it at the time. In my case, closing down emotionally and silently bearing my resentment against my mother was the only way I could deal with her illness.

As an adult, I've been able to work through this issue and let go all of the resentment I was holding against her. Forgiveness can take you into subtle territory - it meant I had to admit to myself how much I had closed down my heart towards her and judged her for being ill. I didn't want to admit my secret inner belief that if she had truly loved us, she would have fought harder to get well.

Forgiveness has also helped me to repair my relationships with other people I've resented over the years like certain friends, teachers, the grumpy man in the local shop, challenging bosses, inconsiderate neighbours, etc.

FORGIVENESS IS POSSIBLE

Even though I don't know the circumstances of your life or who (or what) it is that you want to forgive, I want to assure you that you will be able to do it once you realise what has been in your way. I have successfully coached hundreds of people and every one of them was able to forgive. I've witnessed people authentically forgive every kind of experience including hurt, betrayal, violence, abandonment, physical, emotional and sexual abuse, bullying, unfair treatment, unprovoked attack, deception, intimidation, accidents, significant loss, trauma and even murder, as well as forgiving others for committing suicide and profoundly forgiving themselves.

There are many books, TED talks and articles with inspiring stories of forgiveness. These are usually examples of forgiveness in exceptional and extreme cases, because that's what makes them so impactful and memorable.

For example, Azim Khamisa's only son, Tariq, was shot and killed at age 20 by a fourteen-year old gang member, Tony Hicks, who received a 25-year prison sentence. Azim went on to partner with Tony's grandfather and guardian, Ples Felix, and founded the Tariq Khamisa Foundation – an organisation devoted to 'stopping children from killing children'. However, sometimes stories like these can feel a little disempowering if you are still resistant to forgiving. You might also experience guilt and shame for not feeling able to forgive. But don't worry, by the end of the book you'll have a more compassionate understanding about what's been in your way and how to move beyond it.

Part of what can make forgiveness seem hard is that it's similar to giving up a bad habit. It's something you choose to *stop* doing. If you've ever tried to give up a bad habit it's likely you had a much harder time stopping it than you did starting it up. Letting go of your ill will and resentment works the same way. You need to learn how to drop your hands by your sides and let the burden of all you've been carrying completely fall away.

THE SUPERPOWER OF FORGIVENESS

Forgiveness is like a latent superpower. We all have the capacity to do it, regardless of the circumstances. From what I've learned through watching the almost miraculous changes my clients go through when they fully forgive, there's no downside to letting go of your resentment and forgiving. Yes, you need to take the time and effort to do it, and you will probably experience a little momentary emotional discomfort while you go through the process. But if it means the transformation of a relationship or if you can fully resolve the past, once and for all, then it's totally worth it.

I don't know of any other practice or activity you can do that has the same power and potential to resolve the past that forgiveness has. You can be mindful and meditate fervently for decades and never truly let go of your past and forgive. You can practice non-violent communication skills, and express your needs clearly, but you could still be holding on to your resentment while doing it. You can even have counselling or be in therapy for many years and never forgive a soul.

I'm not suggesting you don't do any of these things. I think all of these techniques are wonderful. But none of them replace the power of refusing to hold your ill will against someone for what they did or didn't do.

According to a Gallup poll on various religious topics, including forgiveness, the report found of those surveyed, "94% said it was important to forgive, but 85% said they needed some outside help to be able to forgive. However, not even regular prayer was found to be effective."

"The need to forgive is widely recognized by the public, but they are often at a loss for ways to accomplish it."

While I wouldn't go quite as far as saying forgiveness is a cure for everything (it won't purify water or heat up your home), it has the potential to radically change your life and the world for the better. Provided that you keep clear boundaries and act for the greatest good of all concerned there are no downsides to it and it's free! There is enormous potential for you to use the superpower of forgiveness to come to a place of peace in yourself, no matter what has happened in your past.

BETTER RELATIONSHIPS

The lack of forgiveness and the harbouring of resentment, guilt, anger, grievances and ranklement, combined with our reluctance to let go of the past, is the cause of most of the problems we have in our relationships. To me, forgiveness is the ultimate relationship detox. Living without resentment is better for you on every level – mental, emotional, physical, spiritual and relational.

Strange and miraculous things can happen after forgiveness. I had one client who, after we'd been through the forgiveness process on her mother, told me that the next day her mother had called her, out of the blue. She told her daughter that she loved her and was proud of her. "She *never* tells me things like that!", she said.

I've had many clients who say they've finally come to peace with the past in just one session. I particularly remember one very courageous woman in her 70s who'd been sexually abused in her teens. At the end of our working together she said, "All of that pain I've been carrying from the past, all of that bad feeling I felt every day, it's all gone!"

I've also worked with many clients who've saved their marriage or intimate partnership through forgiveness because they've finally been able to let go of the build-up of resentment that had been poisoning their relationship for years.

A VISION OF FORGIVENESS

I invite you to put any reservations you might have about forgiveness on hold for a few moments. Whether or not you think you could come to a place of peace with whatever needs to be forgiven in your own life, just allow yourself to use the power of your imagination in this short visualisation:

Imagine you have mastered the art of forgiveness. You are feeling completely and utterly at peace about everyone and everything in your life. You have taken the time to do your work, to resolve every conflict you've ever had and forgiven everyone and everything. There's nothing outstanding left to say, no withholding in your heart. You have made the decision to hold absolutely no ill will against anyone or anything ever again, for any reason.

You feel powerful because you know what's vital for your peace of mind. You feel so at home and so good about yourself and your life that appreciation and kindness flow effortlessly from you towards everyone you meet.

You have clear boundaries. You say "no" firmly and kindly when you need to. You choose how much contact you have with people with whom you've had difficulties in the past. Maybe some of those people aren't in your life any more, but you no longer hold anything against them.

You feel richly connected and free to communicate clearly, openly and deeply with all the people you care about the most. There are no unresolved issues that have been left to fester. Your heart is as open and soft as when you first fall in love.

Imagine the feelings of peace, love, gratitude and appreciation flowing endlessly through your heart, in all your relationships.

How does the rest of your life look from here?

Now imagine that everyone is doing this. Everyone is practicing forgiveness and living with peace in their hearts. There's kindness in every queue, tolerance on the roads, no more cyber-bullying, no more hate crime, just harmony, collaboration, creativity, connection and gratitude everywhere. The friction of creative differences fuels the excitement in collective projects instead of causing conflict.

If anything ever comes up that's challenging or triggers old resentment patterns, everyone takes the time and trouble to notice it. They choose to release any ill will, take the steps necessary to forgive from a clear, open space, and move on.

Can you hear that little voice in your head saying that this is impossible, could never happen and even if it did, life would be boring? This is a glimpse of how you can begin to hear your internal resistance to forgiveness. Sometimes it's hard to even imagine life without resentment in it!

But whether or not you believe it's possible, if (and I know that it's a big if) we each chose this because it's what we want, we could change the world... If *you* choose this, I promise you will change *your* world...

Practice Suggestion: As you read ahead, think and / or write about your personal definition of forgiveness. Think about what you previously thought forgiveness was, as well as what you might understand differently now. How does Brad Brown's definition of forgiveness help you when you think about the person / people you need to forgive?

CHAPTER TWO
FORGIVENESS IS FOR YOU

"Life is an adventure in forgiveness."

Norman Cousins

A TALE OF TWO SAUSAGES
Based on a True Story

Once upon a time, long, long ago, there was a lovely family who lived in a quiet, leafy suburb of London, England.

One Christmas Day, the whole family was gathered around the table for dinner. The eldest daughter was sitting nearest to her father. Sometimes, her table manners didn't meet the required standards of the household and he wanted to be able to reach her with his thin green whacking stick without clipping another member of the family by accident. This had happened the year before and one grandmamma had asked to be moved further down the table this Christmas.

Toward the end of the delicious meal, the eldest daughter balanced her favourite morsels - two mini sausages - on the edge of her plate, keeping the best 'till last, while she finished up the rest of her turkey.

Her eagle-eyed father spotted the sausages. "You don't want those sausages, do you?" he said and popped them both into his mouth before the eldest daughter had a chance to answer.

The young girl was outraged. She turned bright red and shouted at her father, "Hey! I was saving those! Spit them out! They're mine!"

He was so shocked at her reaction that he spat out the half-bitten sausages into his Christmas napkin and apologetically offered them to her. She stood up and burst into angry tears.

The father (who wasn't all bad despite his Victorian ways) said, "I'm sorry, I thought you didn't want them. Sit down. I'll make it up to you!"

But his daughter hissed, "No. And I'll never forgive you for this!" She snatched the Christmas napkin out of his hand and stormed up the stairs to her bedroom.

The mother scowled at the father, "Oh Father...". The middle daughter kept her head down and rubbed her tummy which had just started hurting. The youngest son started to cry because he was frightened by the shouting. One grandmother tutted under her breath and the other shook her head slowly and sighed. Nobody enjoyed their Christmas pudding very much and the afternoon dragged slowly with tension, like indigestion, still in the air.

It was late evening before the eldest daughter would speak to anyone. Only the promise of chocolate liqueurs could tempt her down from her room. She was below the legal age of consumption but these were extreme circumstances.

As soon as she came down the stairs, the father said, "I really am sorry that I ate your sausages. I thought you didn't want them and I should have asked."

"Yes, you should!" she spat.

"Let's make it up?" said the father, with a vague tone of hope in his voice.

"No way!" she said. She grabbed the three largest chocolates and stomped her way loudly back up the stairs. TBC...

FORGIVENESS IS FOR YOU

This book is for you - to help you move beyond your past and truly let go of whatever is troubling you. One of the greatest motivations for forgiveness is knowing that it's you who will be the primary beneficiary when you do it. Forgiveness is for *you*.

You might already know that you want to forgive someone or something from the past that has been a challenge to you in your life. Or there may be a recent event, like the break-up of a relationship, where you know you need to forgive and move on, but you can't. It might be something significant that happened - like a betrayal - or it might be something relatively trivial, like in the story. Or instead, there may be someone you want to forgive *you*. This book can help you with that too. Whichever way, it will feel like something that remains unresolved in you.

THE PAIN YOU'RE IN

When psychotherapists and spiritual teachers Gerry Jampolsky (author of *Love Is Letting Go of Fear*) and his wife Diane Cirincione do their live lectures and workshops they ask their audience to raise their hands if they've totally forgiven their parents. They usually find fewer than half have. And when they ask divorcees if they've completely forgiven their exes, less than 25% of them raise their hands. There's a lot of un-forgiveness even in psychological/spiritual workshops, let alone in the wider world.

Sometimes resentment and anger can be buried so deep you hardly feel it at all. If you've found effective ways of numbing yourself to the stronger emotions like anger, resentment and fear by keeping yourself busy or using food, drugs, TV, or alcohol, you might not feel an urgent need to forgive. But there might be something bothering you that keeps you awake at night. Something that feels like unfinished business lurking way back in the darker corners of your mind. Or you might notice there are habits you want to change, but you can't quite seem to make the shift you want.

You might notice you don't feel so close to your partner or your family or certain friends any more. You might feel as if life itself, or your current circumstances, are against you in some way. Or you might have been the victim of a crime or accident that you can't seem to get over – especially if there have been serious consequences.

Or you might be like I was - faced with a challenging situation that's beyond anyone's control. Then you might not recognize what you're feeling is resentment - because it's overlaid with other feelings, such as guilt, as well. Or you may just be getting on with things, feeling a bit shut-down to the joys of life.

All of these could be subtle signs that there is something inside you that needs to be forgiven.

ACCEPTING THE UNACCEPTABLE

I'm not suggesting that you have to endure terrible circumstances if there's something you can do about them. Sometimes there are changes that can be, and need to be, made in your life. Feeling 'righteous anger' could be a clear indication that some kind of boundary has been transgressed, or there is something that needs to change or stop.

If there's a stand you can take, a protest you can make, or a law you can lobby to change, this can help you to accept the unacceptable. You might be able to take action that will help to create a different future. Anger can be a catalyst for change

This is very different from regretting or wishing something were different in the past or just storing up resentment. Wise action evolves the drive for revenge into the impetus for effective change.

Sometimes, however, there really is nothing you can do about what's happened. One of my clients' teenage sons was attacked from behind by another youth and left permanently disabled. Even after Debra forgave her son's attacker, all of the consequences of her son's physical condition, and the impact it has on their whole family, remained the same. What changed is that she is no longer carrying the weight of anger and resentment around with her in addition to everything else she has to cope with. It's subtle, but vitally important.

"Learning to forgive was the hardest part for me and… the resistance I felt towards it was strong. But what was even more powerful was the guidance I received to break down that barrier. The burden I've been carrying around [with] me for two years sat in the pit of my stomach and I thought I could bury it with food. Oh, how wrong I was. The release was something I have never experienced before. An incredible relief overcame me, and once it lifted, I could then find the right path to forgiveness."

It doesn't matter how much resentment you're carrying or how long you carry it for. Resentment in and of itself, no matter how high you pile it or how long you let it fester, won't make any difference at all to the other person's life, only to yours. If you just suppress your feelings and don't take the steps you need to, your indignation or anger never gets expressed and your resentment is driven underground. One of the steps in my Forgiveness Made Easy process makes room for any feelings like this to be fully expressed.

Refusing to forgive is not the same as setting a boundary although it might feel as if it is. You're perfectly free to keep holding onto your resentment, to seek revenge, blame, invest in games of one-upmanship and have an expensive and acrimonious divorce. Or you could choose to forgive your ex-spouse and divorce anyway (see Katherine Woodward Thomas' book, *"Conscious Uncoupling"*).

One of my clients, Hazel, realised she needed to leave her marriage because she and her husband had grown apart. She was also resentful of her husband's lack of support and frequent criticism of her. She chose to do her forgiveness work on him before she asked for a divorce. Free of her resentment, she was able to clearly and lovingly support them both through the end of their marriage. She was even able to be compassionate and loving towards him in his shock, anger and grief. She went on to create a whole new life for herself, including a new relationship.

You can make powerful, life-changing choices without holding on to any ill will or bad feelings at all.

THE PRICE OF REVENGE

It can be really hard to let go of the feelings inside that demand justice, retribution or revenge. They can feel very intense - like a matter of life or death – because you experience them physiologically as if you're responding to a threat to your survival as opposed to just an emotional upset.

In his article *The Complicated Psychology of Revenge,* Eric Jaffe reports that even though the reward processing centre in the brain that seems to be activated at the thought of revenge (the same part stimulated by cocaine and nicotine use), the act of revenge itself - harming the offender back - doesn't always result in the offended party feeling the issue is resolved.

Other studies have shown that it's only if the person seeking revenge believes the offending party has 'got the message' that the revenge will seem to 'taste sweet'. If the message doesn't seem to have been received there is no sense of closure. In fact, the punisher may dwell on their own act of revenge and feel worse than if they hadn't sought revenge at all.

Another major problem with this attempt at justice is how often the act of vengeance is seen as excessive and needs further retribution, in return. This is how conflicts escalate.

The desire for revenge is not just about the attempt to control someone's behaviour. It can seem as if it will bring the universe back into equilibrium and right a wrong. Of course, revenge doesn't do any of these things in reality. Revenge doesn't resolve an issue. The only way to try to right a wrong is in the making of some kind of amends - restorative justice.

In *Beyond Revenge, the Evolution of the Forgiveness Instinct,* by Michael E McCullough, he suggests that both revenge and forgiveness are evolutionary adaptations for addressing social problems. In the past, before we were able to share ideas in more intelligent ways, revenge might have acted as a deterrent - a way of communicating what is and isn't acceptable social behaviour.

But these studies also found that, thanks to the most evolved part of our brains (the prefrontal cortex), we can override our urges for revenge and choose a more 'social' outcome. They suggest that the capacity for forgiveness (and foregoing vengeance) is an evolutionary development that has helped human beings make the socially beneficial choice to maintain important relationships.

WHY IT'S KILLING YOU NOT TO

What if there was no forgiveness? Just the harbouring of grudges over time and over generations, never ever letting go of anything anyone ever said or did that upset you, always bringing it up with recriminations. No resolution. No chance of inner or outer peace. No way you could ever truly let go and move beyond your past once and for all. You'd be living your whole life in the past. You wouldn't be able to evolve or grow as a person. You'd be hair-trigger reactive to insults and slights and overly sensitive in all social situations. You'd feel stressed and vengeful underneath, all the time... you get the picture.

How about feeling into that right now? Think about someone you've never managed to forgive. Feel into what emotions are subtly present in your body if you put your attention on them. What's the emotional cocktail in there? Is it anger, sorrow, fear, desire for revenge, hate, resentment, indignation, fury? Feel into it all. Here it all is, alive in you, present right now, and you can notice it just by putting your attention on it, not very far under the surface, just waiting to be resolved.

Then let yourself become aware of your thoughts and any added meaning you're giving your situation. What's that little voice in your head telling you? "They're wrong. They should apologise....", "If they treat me like that, then they....", "If I forgive them, then....", "I can't allow myself to look....", "I have to....", "If only they would....", "Life is...." These (often un-noticed) interpretations of the events of our lives - what I'll call 'meaning making'- can be part of what gets in the way of forgiveness. I'll say more about why this is so critical to your ability to forgive later on.

Carrying resentment doesn't only have an impact on your mental and emotional health. The latest discoveries in neuroscience prove an undeniable relationship between what we think, what we feel and the physical state of our bodies. Dr L Wilson says: "Resentment kills. Holding on to anger and holding grudges wears out the adrenal glands and the thyroid gland. Eventually, it weakens the entire body and mind."

Having significant, unresolved emotional issues (or even just some little niggles that are ongoing) will affect how you feel about yourself, others and your life. The emotional stress might show up in other ways. You may feel more anxious, less able to cope with crises, easily triggered and more 'emotional' than you'd like to be.

Any kind of conflict or unresolved issue remains an incomplete or 'open loop' to your brain. Your brain is constantly tracking everything you do and you're hardwired to find the things you've lost and come to terms with the past. When things are left incomplete you can never truly be at peace. This leaves major neurobiological and psychological sources of stress active inside you and in the long term these will take their toll on your health as well as on your peace of mind.

It's pretty widely known that stress kills. Latest reports show it to be implicated in 75% of all doctor visits in the USA. Carrying resentment is carrying stress 24/7 even if you're not consciously aware of it.

Another research paper, *How the Brain Heals Emotional Wounds; the Functional Neuroanatomy of Forgiveness* stated: "Negative affect and chronic emotional distress erode health (Hu and Gruber, 2008), impoverish sleep quality (Stoia-Caraballo et al. 2008), stimulate the production of stress-related hormones, such as cortisol (Berry and Worthington, 2001), being associated over time with the development of clinical conditions such as depression (e.g. Nolen-Hoeksema and Morrow, 1991)."

As well as the obvious emotional advantages of living resentment-free, forgiveness is beginning to be associated with a whole range of health benefits. The practice of forgiveness is associated with a reduction in physical symptoms, reduced heart rate, increased well-being, increased cardiovascular health, reduced reliance on alcohol, drugs and medications and may increase longevity; "The fact that forgiving is a healthy resolution of the problems caused by injuries suggests that this process might have evolved as a favourable response that promotes human survival."

The authors of the study made a distinction between what they call "trait forgiveness" and "state forgiveness" – suggesting you can live your life with a generally forgiving attitude towards others or you can decide to forgive only in a specific circumstance.

I think it's even better to do both. Ideally you will have a powerful intention not to carry your grudges around with you from the past *and* have a forgiveness practice and process that you use whenever you realise you are starting to gather new grievances against someone and want to let them go.

THE VIEW FROM THE BALCONY

Forgiveness involves an internal mind-shift. It includes changing your perspective and challenging your assumptions and the meaning you've given past events. This ability to 'refresh your browser' and change your attitude is a conscious move you can make away from the ancient part of your brain that will be urging you to get revenge to the saner, prefrontal cortex that is able to see the bigger picture and make a better choice. This can be hard to do in the heat of the moment, but you can develop this capacity by practicing forgiveness (and meditation). You'll notice the difference in your peace of mind, your health, how well you sleep at night and maybe even in the lightness of your heart too.

Negotiation expert William Ury calls this kind of internal mind-shift in perception 'going to the balcony'. This is a metaphor for, "a mental and emotional place of perspective, calm and self-control", where you take a higher, wider perspective. It's as if you're looking over a drama that's being acted out on a stage and where you can see everything including yourself and your part in the play.

Choosing to accept the unacceptable (like the tragedy of Debra's son's attack) can become a little easier from the balcony because you see the events in your life in context, as part of the entire play. When challenging events happen, taking this perspective can help you to take the events of life less personally and keep focused on what's most important.

When my son was due to be born I had prepared and planned to have a natural birth at home. I breathed and chanted my way, drug free, through 24 hours of labour, supported with frequent back rubs from my partner. But when the midwife came the second time she discovered that the baby was in an undiagnosed breech position, so I wasn't allowed to continue my labour at home.

My partner took me straight to the hospital. I was shocked and felt as if I was in a terrible dream. After another 12 hours of labour I ended up needing an emergency caesarean section to save the baby's life when his heart-rate plunged dangerously low. What was most important, from the perspective of the bigger picture, was the health and safety of the baby and me, rather than whether or not I successfully carried out my ideal natural birth plan.

Knowing how to forgive meant that I was able to let go of any bad feelings I was holding against myself, the baby and the medical staff for not diagnosing his position earlier. Then I could just accept the circumstances for what they were and be grateful for the safe delivery of a beautiful, healthy boy.

RESOLVING THE PAST

Spiritual teacher Thomas Huebl says that unresolved emotional difficulties never go away until you take the time to face them. He says they're like pop-ups on your screen that you keep clicking to close, but they keep on popping back up, until you finally feel ready to face and resolve them.

Until you become curious about how forgiveness can be like a superpower in your life, you're not likely to proactively do your forgiveness work. It will never seem to be an urgent priority. If you find out the person you've been resenting for years has a fatal illness and will die in the next few weeks, perhaps you'll be inspired to do it then. Otherwise, you could end up carrying your resentment to your grave.

I've worked with many clients who've done their forgiveness work on family members and friends who have already died. What's amazing and wonderful about the Forgiveness Made Easy process is that it works equally well whether the person you want to forgive is alive or dead, estranged from you or sleeping next to you in your bed. It also works equally well for recently gathered grievances and resentment you've been carrying all your life. The only difference is if you've been carrying your resentment over months, years or decades, the process may take slightly longer, too.

Dr Christiane Northrup writes in her book, *The Wisdom of Menopause,* that unresolved trauma resurfaces around the time of menopause. She says, "The primary defence against unpleasant memories and emotions is avoidance. This subterfuge often works reasonably well until the perimenopausal transition when the hormonal shift of focus and accompanying changes in brain activity conspire to call buried traumas and unresolved issues into the light, expressing them through physical symptoms that cannot be ignored."

This doesn't mean you need to wait until you're having a mid-life crisis to work on letting go. Nor does it mean it's too late for you if you are past middle age. Or, if you're not a woman, that you're exempt from this hormonally-driven opportunity. Anyone can do forgiveness work whenever they like. The most important point here is that most of us will want to avoid it, everyone needs to do it and everyone can benefit from their own forgiveness.

Dr Northrup also advocates for forgiveness: "Ultimately, make it your goal to move on to forgiveness of yourself and those involved in causing you pain in the past. Forgiveness doesn't mean that what happened to you was acceptable. It simply means that you are no longer willing to allow a past injury to keep you from living fully and healthfully in the present."

Forgiveness is for everyone It's not reserved only for those who have experienced significant trauma. Forgiveness is for every circumstance with no exceptions. Forgiveness is not just for resolving the past. Forgiveness is a principle for life.

TRULY LETTING GO

So far as I know, it's impossible to actually go back in time and change the events of your past (other than in your imagination.) You need to give up the hope of having had a happier or a different past and accept that what happened, *happened*, however traumatic or tragic. And then you have to bring the past to the present to resolve it. There isn't any other way of doing it.

I think of this as the 'liquid edge' of reality. Everything before this moment has solidified – it's the past, it's happened, it's over. The liquid edge is where you have the power and flexibility to change your current circumstances. Even if that power is limited, you at least have the power to change your attitude and your perspective about what is happening now. This applies even when 'what is happening' is you remembering and coming to terms with your past.

Once you've changed your perspective by going to the balcony, you might also be able to make a new choice to move in another direction, to create a different, more inspiring future. But sometimes, facing a painful past means just being willing to completely and utterly accept things were the way they were. Of course, this is likely to be much easier to say than to do.

If you're seven years old and your parents send you away to boarding school, you may believe that it was something you said or did 'wrong' - even if they never told you anything of the sort. It's likely you won't have had the emotional maturity at the time to say much about it or feel as if you had any power over the decision that was being made on your behalf. You might come to terms with your parents' decision as you get older and you may even come to appreciate some of the benefits of your education. You might also carry resentment against your parents about it for the rest of your life until you realise you need to forgive them.

When you have been hurt by someone, understanding why they did or didn't do something can be helpful. When I work with clients and we go back in time to something that needs to be forgiven from their childhood, often the question they most want to ask is "Why...?" But understanding alone isn't a substitute for forgiveness.

Forgiveness is the only way to find true resolution and completion not just for your past, but also in your on-going relationships. Forgiveness has the power to help you free yourself from any negative childhood behaviour patterns that may still be sabotaging your happiness or success as an adult. If you choose to forgive, you can create a new future for yourself that would otherwise be impossible if you didn't find a way to let go of your anger, pain, guilt, grievances, and the past.

As Viktor Frankl, a prisoner in Auschwitz, wrote: "When we are no longer able to change a situation, we are challenged to change ourselves."

THE MAGIC PILL

Forgiveness is the master practice of letting go. Forgiveness has the potential to transform every single relationship you have now (especially the tricky ones) and every relationship you will have in the future, as well as resolve every past relationship issue you've ever had. It could even help prevent divorce, resolve family feuds, improve your mental, emotional and physical health and change how you feel about yourself. Ultimately it has the power to transform the world.

Imagine for a moment there was a magic pill you could take that guaranteed similarly miraculous results. As soon as you take it you begin to feel:

- ✓ Lighter than you have in years
- ✓ Happier than you can remember
- ✓ Like you want to be more loving to all the people in your life

Taking this pill could improve every single relationship you have:

- ✓ With your family of origin
- ✓ Your co-workers and colleagues
- ✓ Your spouse
- ✓ Your kids
- ✓ Your friends
- ✓ Your pets
- ✓ Your spiritual life
- ✓ Yourself

And not only that, this pill would be able to:

- ✓ Reach places that other therapies have never reached
- ✓ Resolve past trauma that you may have so far failed to let go

In addition, this magic pill had been tested and shown to:

- ✓ Enhance your ability to problem solve
- ✓ Give you access to greater creativity through changing your brain state
- ✓ Develop characteristics associated with leadership

The physical 'side effects' of taking this magic pill are that it helps:

- ✓ Lower your levels of cortisol (the stress hormone)
- ✓ Reduce your risk of heart attack

- ✓ Lower your blood pressure
- ✓ Improve weight loss
- ✓ Overcome depression
- ✓ Make you feel less anxious
- ✓ Feel less tension in your body
- ✓ Sleep better at night
- ✓ Even die a peaceful death – with no emotional baggage left outstanding

Regular use of this pill would result in you:

- ✓ Feeling more freedom and peace within yourself
- ✓ Feeling more connected to all the other people in your life
- ✓ Being more successful in your business relationships
- ✓ Having a better experience of sex and your erotic life

And this pill wouldn't just benefit you, but the knock-on effects would:

- ✓ Help change the culture of cyber-bullying and hate crime
- ✓ Help create peaceful societies
- ✓ Ultimately help to create global peace

Would you take it?

You'd probably order several bottles or get the 'buy two, get one free' offer and share it with all your friends! You'd want everyone to take it with you... You'd be crazy not to!

Am I saying that forgiveness has all the phenomenal potential of that magic pill?

Yes.

Maybe you want to re-read that list again? Would you take the pill? I'm hoping that your answer is "yes" and that you're at least a little curious about how you can receive all of these benefits for yourself.

If your answer is "maybe" - or even "no" - that's OK too. That's partly why I wrote this book. The power of forgiveness is utterly transformational, so the fact that we're not all queuing up to do it means there must be *really* convincing reasons why not. Why isn't it taught in schools and offered as part of our health services? Why isn't it part of our everyday lives?

Our evolutionary biology has programmed human beings with a tendency to seek pleasure, avoid pain and do whatever seems to be the easiest thing. The fact that we tend to *not* choose forgiveness suggests that we need another way to look at forgiveness - as a new wonder-supplement – and make it easy to do.

So what else besides our natural proclivity for revenge is getting in the way? That's what we'll look into next.

Practice Suggestion: Think or journal about what your reasons are for wanting to forgive and list any symptoms you can notice that suggest you may not have completely forgiven someone/something. If you're feeling worried about the idea of forgiveness, write down all the reservations you have and what you're afraid might happen if you did forgive.

PART TWO
WHY IT'S HARD

"Forgiveness is giving up all hope for a better past."

Corinne Edwards after Gerald Jampolsky

CHAPTER THREE
WHY IS IT SO HARD?

"We especially need to forgive each other because
when you intend to forgive, you heal part of the pain,
but when you forgive, you heal completely."

Nelson Mandela

A TALE OF TWO SAUSAGES ...cont.

The following year, the family gathered again at the Christmas table.
The eldest daughter sat down next to her father in her usual place.
When everyone was settled, she pulled out last year's crumpled-up
Christmas napkin from her pocket and laid it on the table.

Slowly, she unwrapped the little parcel and pulled out two hardened,
mould covered, half-bitten sausages and placed them between her
and her father. A terrible odour filled the air. Then she put her hand
into her other pocket and pulled out some other mouldering things
and piled them up with the sausages into a little wall.

She didn't need to say anything. Her father had got the point. The
whole family had got the point. The delicious Christmas dinner was
spoiled. TBC...

YOU'RE NORMAL

Forgiveness is challenging for many reasons. You can get tripped
up by one thing, or a combination of things, because there are

stumbling blocks every step of the way. But like every worthwhile pursuit, there are massive gains to be made as you go through your journey of forgiveness.

Any trouble you're having is not personal to you. Struggling to forgive is a universal problem. Not only that, but forgiveness is counter-culture. There are far more popular stories and movies that include the theme of revenge than there are about forgiveness. The movie with the infamous line, "Don't get mad, forgive" was never made.

Also, forgiveness may not seem like a very attractive proposition unless you understand that it's like a martial art for the heart - something that can develop powerful qualities and strengths within you. Even if you associate forgiveness with inspiring spiritual teachers and leaders like Gandhi, Nelson Mandela and the Dalai Lama, it can still seem like forgiveness will make you vulnerable and put you in a weaker position. You may think you aren't going to get very far in life if you just back down and let people off the hook all the time.

You're also not likely to leap into any kind of activity if you don't really know what it is, why you're doing it, who's going to benefit from it or when and how to do it. No wonder there's not much forgiveness going on!

WHAT IT IS

You've already overcome what is often the very first stumbling block – misunderstanding exactly what forgiveness is and isn't. Just to re-iterate, forgiveness is not condoning or overlooking unacceptable behaviour, it's not about lying down and letting everyone walk all over you. Forgiveness is just the absolute refusal to hold onto your ill will / grudge / grievance / anger / rancour / resentment (however you want to say it) and the past. It's the simple and profound act of letting go. It's the great undoing.

WHY

Forgiveness releases you from the past. It's impossible to hold on and let go of something at the same time. Forgiveness is the only cure for resentment and is probably the highest expression of love there is. The trouble is, we don't always notice when we need to forgive, especially if the other person is obviously just plain *wrong.* Sometimes it's difficult to admit you need to forgive and let go. We also don't like to think of ourselves as resentful people. It's not something you'll add to your on-line dating profile: "I bear grudges for a long time and never let people forget when they've let me down..." Not very sexy.

Sometimes what we feel about other people is ambivalent or contradictory. We might be grateful for everything our parents did for us, while also wishing they'd done some of it differently.

My father used to call us 'stupid' if we did anything wrong or messed something up. He'd say, "You're stupid! What are you...?" To which we were required to respond, "Stupid, Daddy."

That programming had a significant impact on my behaviour. I would try to know everything to avoid ever looking stupid and I'd be reluctant to take significant risks in case I got something wrong again. Even though my father was marvellous in many ways, and there is so much that I'm grateful to him for, I did need to forgive him for that part of his legacy (amongst other things.)

Often, we're unaware that what we're carrying *is* resentment. I remember working with one client who said she didn't need to forgive the grandmother who'd protected her during her abusive childhood. As we worked through her process, however, she realised that she was holding huge resentment against her grandmother because of the control she'd had over the whole family and the decisions her grandmother made that had affected my client's early life. The territory of forgiveness is not always clear cut. What is true, though, is that we will *always* benefit when we do forgive.

WHO IT'S FOR

Forgiveness is always for you. Many people are blithely unaware of the enormous costs of not having resolved the past. If a relationship is suffering because of the build-up of resentment, forgiveness can help to resuscitate it. If the relationship is over and you still can't let go of something that happened – forgiveness is the only true route to resolution. However many years of therapy you do first, peace will only flow through your heart when you've finally forgiven. I've worked with many people who've said, "I've never been there before" because through the superpower of forgiveness, they've finally found a way to resolve something in the past that has been eluding them for years if not decades.

WHEN TO DO IT

There's a very famous spiritual teacher who, when one of his students asked him how many times he had to forgive his brother, recommended that he do it 490 times! (70 x 7). I think what Jesus was saying is that you have to forgive every time something comes up that needs to be forgiven. Every time you become aware you're holding a grudge, or your heart has contracted or closed down a little. Every time. You might also need to speak up as well – forgiving is not about being a wuss - you can do both.

If you stay conscious of what's happening in the moment as it occurs, especially if you 'go to the balcony' and take a higher perspective, you can avoid letting your unexpressed grievances, judgements and anger solidify into resentment.

HOW TO DO IT

Another reason why forgiveness is hard is because it's not something we're taught how to do. Even in the most inspiring books on forgiveness, there is often an assumption that you know what forgiveness is and how to do it. Even when there are processes or steps offered, the actual mechanics of *how* to do the forgiveness part is usually just 'forgive them'.

This lack of clear how-to guidance is one of the main reasons why I've written this book. I want to share how to overcome the most common obstacles to forgiveness, together with some other ideas that can help you feel much more ready, willing and able to forgive. I also want to share a forgiveness process that is powerful, authentic and can change your life - as opposed to just begrudgingly saying "I forgive you" through gritted teeth, with little conviction or sincerity and while still maintaining a firm grip on your resentment!

COGNITIVE BIASES

Human beings are 'meaning-making machines'. Most of the time the 'reality' we're living in is our interpretation of events rather than what's actually happening. When you walk into a room and everyone goes silent, you immediately think it's got something to do with you rather than assuming they're all taking a minute's silence in honour of someone who just died or any number of other perfectly legitimate reasons. Your version is there's something wrong with you, they all hate you or they're planning to sack you. A lot of soap opera drama is based on people getting the wrong end of the stick and secrets that get withheld until a big disclosure episode.

Everyone suffers from inaccurate thinking at times. If you're interested, check out the list of 102 cognitive biases on Wikipedia. This is a list of 102 different ways you can deceive yourself; such as "the identifiable victim effect" – where you're more likely to send money to help a particular person at risk than to a large group of people at risk.

I remember one time being on the Underground in London and asking one of the guards on a train if it was going to the destination I wanted. I didn't board the train because I thought what he told me was wrong. He wasn't of course!

We all have a tendency to misinterpret events and take offence when none may have been intended. Everyone is judging, commentating on, and trying to make sense of the world - whatever we can do to help us feel more in control of our increasingly fast-paced modern lives.

You may not always be mistaken in your interpretation of events and I'm not dismissing that challenging things may have happened to you. It's important to honour the past by telling the truth about it. But there is also the possibility that you may have assigned additional meaning to that event, or made it mean something about you that isn't true, which has added to your suffering. For example, if someone is abusive or has betrayed your trust, you might have interpreted their behaviour to mean you don't matter to them or you're unlovable or unworthy in some way. This kind of suffering – the rain from beneath your own umbrella – gets relieved as part of your forgiveness process.

YOUR EVOLUTIONARY INHERITANCE

You are evolutionarily programmed to take more notice of negative information and experiences than of positive ones. This is the so-called 'negativity bias'. It's obvious that you need to be more wary of a stick that looks like it could be a snake, and not step on it, rather than to make a potentially fatal mistake and step forward carelessly onto a snake hoping it's going to be a stick. This bias will have ensured our survival over generations. But it also means you have to make an effort to overcome that bias. You have to give yourself extra time to really take in and appreciate the positive moments in your life.

Nowadays, most of the stress you're under is likely to be from challenging social or emotional circumstances rather than because you're in physical danger. But whatever the stressor, your body will react the same way. If you're in a social situation where you think you're being excluded, your brain will respond as though you were in physical danger and bypass the more recently evolved prefrontal cortex.

This is partly good news because it's the same mechanism that will get you out of the path of an oncoming vehicle without you having to work out how to do it. You'll just move – *fast*. It will save your life sometimes. It's just that most of the time, when it comes to matters of forgiveness, your life isn't at stake – it's only your self-image and reputation. I'll say more about how all of this plays out in chapter five when we'll take a closer look at the workings of the ego in relation to why we don't forgive.

When you've just been triggered by something that you respond to with anger, the part of your brain that wants to ensure your survival will bypass your pre-frontal cortex. It's as if the part of your brain that governs your pro-social behaviour, like empathy, compassion and forgiveness, gets switched to another channel - the part of you that wants to retaliate or get revenge. That's why it's almost impossible to forgive in the heat of the moment.

In addition to all of this, the most ancient part of your brain which is programmed for your survival actually filters vital information. In the famous *'Selective Attention'* test (if you haven't seen it, check out the YouTube video - see notes for the link), just the simple act of putting your attention on one thing, means you're likely to miss other information. This means when you're resenting someone, your mind might be distorting your opinion of who they are, by emphasising their bad points or focusing only on everything they do that irritates you.

In Professor Steve Peter's self-help bestseller, *The Chimp Paradox*, he uses the metaphor of a chimp to represent the part of the brain that takes over to guarantee our survival. He says that once the chimp is in charge, there's no point trying to reason with it until it's calmed down. You can't put it back in its cage and give it a banana until it's finished its tantrum...

This isn't to say that all anger is 'bad' – Robert Augustus Masters says in his book, *Spiritual Bypassing* "As much as anger can injuriously burn, it can also illuminate; it all depends on what kind of relationship with anger we choose to cultivate."

Feeling anger can have a positive outcome if it precipitates some kind of beneficial change to a challenging situation. If there is injustice that triggers your anger, that feeling may help you to take action. Anger often arises when we have reached our limit of tolerance - or even exceeded it. Then anger can be the impetus to make a change. This doesn't mean you have to express your anger in the heat of the moment. It is possible to notice the feeling of anger flowing through your body as it's happening, take a moment or two of space and then make a conscious choice how to respond.

Viktor Frankl knew this fundamental truth, too, "Between stimulus and response, there is a space. In that space is our power to choose our response. In our response lies our growth and our freedom."

WHY NOT FORGIVE?

Forgiveness is always possible. You still might not be convinced yet, but bear with me. There are three other significant and persistent obstacles that you need to be aware of that will help to make it easy – that's what we'll cover next. All of these obstacles are scaleable. As you go through the coming chapters and face each one of these difficulties and reservations about forgiveness, they will dissolve. By the time you get to the Forgiveness Made Easy process, you will be well prepared and willing, maybe even eager to do it.

Practice Suggestion: As you read ahead, think of or write down in your journal the name of at least one person that you know you need to do your work on. Feel into your feelings, listen to your thoughts and see if you can take yourself to the balcony whilst you do this, as if you are looking at yourself and the situation from a higher perspective. See if anything looks different from there. Make any relevant notes.

CHAPTER FOUR
VULNERABILITY

*"In the final analysis, the goal of every person
is simply peace of mind."*

His Holiness the Dalai Lama

One of the main reasons we resist the idea of forgiveness is because it brings up feelings of intense vulnerability. Being vulnerable can feel so unbearable we will do whatever we can to avoid it. Why does it feel so vulnerable to forgive? Is it natural or is it a cultural thing? In order to make forgiveness easy, you need to become aware of the relationship between vulnerability and the fear of forgiveness and some of the most common misunderstandings and beliefs around it.

Vulnerability, like forgiveness, is also prone to being misunderstood. This is because there are two primary ways of looking at vulnerability; one that you may resist which will hinder you if you want to forgive, and another way that may help you.

VULNERABILITY AND SURVIVAL

The word vulnerability has its Latin roots in the word to "wound". To be vulnerable means you are open to being wounded. And this is true. Being a human being is a tender, temporary, even fragile thing. Just think about it – if your heart stops beating, or you stop breathing for more than a few minutes, your body will die.

But when we talk about vulnerability, we don't usually mean we're afraid for our physical survival – we usually mean emotional vulnerability. Fear of vulnerability is the fear of being hurt or exposed emotionally, of opening ourselves up to the possibility of experiencing pain. It's the fear of making mistakes or being wrong in some way. It's the fear of being taken advantage of. And it's the fear of being seen exactly as we are - all we are and all we are not.

Life itself is fundamentally unpredictable and uncontrollable, other people equally so. Most of us want to feel safe, comfortable and in control more than anything else. Living your life with your heart open to everything, at all times, no matter what is going on, would be a profound expression of vulnerability. It would also seem like the ultimate in emotional risk-taking, especially if you have been the victim of abuse or trauma in the past. We're often not conscious of the drives for security, safety, comfort and control that run our behaviour, but they're ever present in all of us. It's no wonder we want to avoid situations where we might feel vulnerable. You're probably not going to voluntarily make your life uncertain and unpredictable unless you love variety and living on the edge!

Your survival instincts will drive you to fight, flee or freeze when confronted with danger. Even if it's 'emotional danger' your behaviour will be broadly the same. When something happens that makes you feel emotionally vulnerable you'll usually react in one of three ways. You'll become:

- Angry, attacking and defensive
- Accommodating and appeasing or
- Withdraw, go cold and try to avoid the problem altogether.

You might try one approach and then another. For instance, if you back down and try to appease someone, you might get angry later on if it doesn't give you the result you want.

In Brené Brown's excellent book, *Daring Greatly – How the Courage to be Vulnerable Transforms the Way We Live, Love, Parent and Lead,* she says, "To feel is to be vulnerable... I define vulnerability as uncertainty, risk and emotional exposure." She goes on to say that this cultural interpretation of vulnerability is what leads us to associate all of our inner emotions and feelings with weakness, with the exception of anger, which 'feels' strong. This is why holding on to resentment can feel powerful and the idea of letting it go can feel weak.

This association between our survival instincts and our fear of vulnerability affects all of our relationships and the depth to which we feel our emotions, and this is why it's so relevant to forgiveness.

VULNERABILITY AND POWER

When you were younger, you might have felt you had no power to challenge someone with authority over you like a parent, teacher or respected community member. You might have learned that it wasn't safe to answer back or say how you felt at the time. You might have had no say at all in certain events that changed your life. You may have felt as if you had little or no power of your own.

In circumstances where you've felt powerless, your resentment might seem like the only thing you have to hold onto. It can act like a protective shield that you can immediately erect around yourself as a defence against serious abuse, damage, harm, trauma, accident, or tragedy.

Brad Brown calls resentment "The power of the powerless." This is one of the main reasons we don't want to forgive, because it feels like we'll be giving up this illusion of power.

I say illusion of power because it isn't really power at all. However much resentment you carry, it won't and can't change the circumstances of your past. You might think your resentment is communicating something to the other person about what upset you and how you're feeling. Or that it will inspire enough remorse and shame in them that they change, repent or at least apologise. But, in reality, the shut-down is only happening inside you. The other person might be completely unaware that they did anything to upset you or that you're experiencing some emotional distress.

Even if you're not in any actual danger, the idea of forgiving someone can feel like you'll be putting yourself in a disadvantageous position - as if you will be backing down or saying something is OK with you when it's definitely not. But forgiveness is *never* about condoning unacceptable behaviour. Forgiveness is simply a choice about whether or not you hold onto your ill will about something or someone.

It may well be that the other person's behaviour is challenging, abusive or unacceptable to you. However, the truth is, you are powerless to change other people's behaviour. The only chess piece in the game of life that you have complete control over is your own.

Before you feel able to forgive someone, you may need to connect with the power and autonomy of your adult self, so that you feel strong enough inside to be willing to let go of the past and ask for what you need.

VULNERABILITY AND STRENGTH

In the absence of any other strategy, you might use holding on to your resentment as a way to create some emotional distance between yourself and the other person. This might feel like a smart move – like an act of strength. It might seem to solve the problem of how you can be in an ongoing relationship with your family of origin or with bosses, colleagues, your partner or your kids, when there are toxic elements at play between you.

You might be a little less warm towards someone and your body language may be more closed down. You may speak in a particular way, in tone or volume, or restrict the length or depth of your communication. This often feels safer than speaking up and saying what's wrong and facing either an outburst of anger or some other threat, like violence or a verbal attack. The risk of triggering someone else's disapproval can be enough to make you behave in distorted ways and not be honest and authentic. But this kind of behaviour is not true strength and doesn't stop you from being vulnerable to the other person's behaviour. It is an illusion of action and strength.

VULNERABILITY AND JUSTICE

You're also likely to feel vulnerable if you think the other person is getting away with something they shouldn't. Everyone has this in-built sense of justice about what's right and what's acceptable behaviour from others - even when we're not always living up to our own standards! We want things to be fair and forgiveness doesn't seem to balance the scales that have already tipped against us.

I'm sure you've noticed that life *isn't* fair. Trying to even up the balance by exacting revenge or harbouring resentment doesn't actually make you less vulnerable. Holding onto your resentment prolongs the agony because the knife stays in the wound and the injury can never heal. You will be hypersensitive to any knocks that happen near where the knife is planted and could end up feeling even *more* vulnerable.

VULNERABILITY AND DANGER

Forgiveness is not about making yourself deliberately vulnerable in dangerous situations. If there is any danger - get out. It's not about letting people get away with abusive behaviour. It's not about forgetting or overlooking it either.

If you had any adverse childhood experiences, particularly ones that were seriously abusive, you may have felt as if your life was in danger and you may have made some smart decisions to stop you from getting into similar situations again. Our survival instincts programme the brain to remember the danger we've been in so that we don't repeat the pattern. But these self-protective behaviour patterns from childhood can be emotionally debilitating in adult life especially if the pattern never evolves into a healthy adult coping mechanism. The brain will always prioritise your survival even if it has to temporarily sacrifice your psychological wellbeing in the process.

The latest brain science research shows the potent negative impact of adverse childhood experiences especially in relation to your physical health. In *Childhood Disrupted*, Donna Nakazawa states that significant emotional upset can have more of a negative effect on the child than a physical trauma. But the important distinction to make is that as an adult, any *emotional* danger you might feel will not be life-threatening.

Whatever your childhood experiences may have been, they will have impacted how you feel about vulnerability in general. Your childhood coping mechanisms will stay operational until you do something consciously to change and upgrade them.

The truth about vulnerability is that it takes incredible strength to allow yourself to be vulnerable and authentic with others. Seeing vulnerability as a strength is not how we usually view it. 'True' vulnerability is a kind of emotional strength that allows you to show when you are moved by the experiences of your life. You express yourself authentically and allow yourself to be seen exactly as you are. Being vulnerable in this way, would be like admitting when you don't know something rather than pretending that you do. Or saying how you really feel, when everyone else around you is saying something different. It's being honest when you're in pain, angry, mistaken or grieving a loss.

There may be certain circumstances where being vulnerable even as an adult could be inappropriate or threaten your well-being. But in the right situations, allowing yourself to be vulnerable, means that you can be open hearted, authentic, responsive and more sensitive and aware in your interactions with others.

VULNERABILITY AND FEELING YOUR FEELINGS

Vulnerability is all about your relationship with your feelings. It can be hard even to admit you've been hurt or upset by something that someone said, did, or didn't do. Most of us aren't taught how to cope with our really powerful feelings. We don't know how to express them or how to let ourselves feel them fully. We're lucky if we have had good role models for this. You may have been trained to shut down your feelings, or been cautioned with: "Stop crying, or I'll give you something to cry about," or "Big boys don't cry."

It's natural to want to avoid feeling bad. Everything in your physiology is evolutionarily programmed to avoid pain and seek pleasure. But *avoiding* feeling your feelings, like pain, loss, disappointment or hurt, means that you have to live with all the emotional and physiological stress of unexpressed emotions and unresolved situations.

If you feel angry, or hurt or vengeful, you have to start where you are and accept and include those feelings. As Archbishop Desmond Tutu says of forgiveness, "It's also a process that does not exclude hatred and anger."

Anger often arises because there has been a boundary transgression e.g. someone takes something that belongs to you or you've asked someone to stop behaving in a particular way, and they've ignored or forgotten your request. Forgiveness doesn't require you to abandon your boundaries. And there's no justification for abusive, cruel or violent behaviour.

Sometimes, when the circumstances are beyond everyone's control, there isn't anywhere to lay the blame. I felt I couldn't be outwardly angry about my mother's illness. I didn't know how to handle the pain of her physical and psychological decline without withdrawing into myself and shutting down the painful feelings. But the feelings didn't go away until I did my forgiveness work about my mother many years later.

In my experience, the *only* way I've ever seen an issue get properly, once-and-for-all resolved, is by fully facing it on every level, including feeling all the feelings that are associated with it and letting go of any ill will. This means being willing to allow yourself to be 'truly' vulnerable.

If you want anything in your life to change, you have to meet your circumstances exactly the way they *are* first, even if it feels deeply uncomfortable. Many of my clients have said that it was better to experience a shorter, relatively intense few moments of fully feeling their feelings, while in a safe context, than to continue carrying the chronic unresolved resentment and stress around with them.

Vulnerability means being willing to feel all of your feelings, not just the ones you'd prefer to feel. For instance, you could be reluctant to allow yourself to feel compassion towards yourself for the terrible things that have happened to you in your life. If you open up to that feeling of tenderness towards yourself, you will also have to admit to the pain you were in at the time. Sometimes this can be hard to bear. But by being willing to face what you need to face and allowing yourself to feel and express whatever is arising in you that is unresolved, you can clear and resolve it completely. I'll say more about how this works in the Forgiveness Made Easy process itself.

VULNERABILITY AND THE FINER FEELINGS

The trouble with wanting to shut down or limit your vulnerability is that you also risk minimising your experience of your finer feelings - the more sublime end of the emotional spectrum.

The true meaning of vulnerability is more than just the ability to be wounded. It includes the capacity to be open to, moved and affected by all the events and experiences of your life. You are vulnerable when you allow yourself to be touched by life. It's in how your heart responds and opens to a moving piece of music, a magical moment of tenderness or a beautiful vista as much as by the challenges and tribulations of life.

In her book *Daring Greatly,* Brené Brown says that we most often associate vulnerability with only the 'negative' emotions like sadness, shame, grief, fear and disappointment. But vulnerability is also the opening to love, courage, empathy, creativity, joy, belonging, happiness and hope, too.

Being vulnerable allows you to feel all your feelings – good, bad, and everything in between. However powerful, however vague or indistinct - the intense and specific rushes of desire, the heart-unfurling of love, the swelling of pride, the snakes of jealousy, the furnace of anger, the giddiness of joy, the overflowing of gratitude, the contraction of pain, the delicacy of hope and the ominous chords of fear – all of them are universal and all of them enrich your precious experience of living life to the full.

As Kahlil Gibran wrote in *The Prophet:* "And could you keep your heart in wonder at the daily miracles of your life, your pain would not seem less wondrous than your joy."

If you want to be able to have rich, fulfilling, authentic relationships, you have to be willing to risk being vulnerable. Brené Brown says, "Vulnerability is the core, the heart, the centre, of meaningful human experiences." Vulnerability is the heart of true intimacy.

CONNECTING OR SEPARATING EMOTIONS

There's no need to be afraid of your feelings – even the ones that make you feel separate from other people like fear, anger, jealousy, shame, and hate. Just like powerful waves on the sea, the pure intensity of your emotions will rise and fall. Think about what happens when you let yourself have a good cry. There comes a point when the upset subsides, before you feel another wave of sadness rise and your sobs increase again. Viewed over time, your emotional experience may seem more like the tides, changing with the different phases and major and minor events of your life.

I learned from Brad Brown, co-founder of the More to Life programme, a useful way of distinguishing between the emotions you like and the ones you'd prefer not to feel. Rather than calling your feelings 'positive or negative' you see them as either 'separating' you from yourself, others and life or 'connecting' you to yourself, others and life. For example, heart-opening feelings like joy and happiness will help you to feel connected with others, whereas heart-closing emotions like jealousy, envy or guilt will tend to make you feel separate. Emotions like sadness or grief, because they are heart-opening feelings, can be incredibly connecting. This is why there are so many sad songs out there – they connect us in our deepest vulnerabilities.

This is not to say you'll necessarily want to reach out to others when you're grieving or feeling really sad. I'm just inviting you to become more aware of the subtle movements of your heart, so you can live a happier, freer life. Just notice as you go through the pages of this book which thoughts and memories evoke 'heart-opening' feelings and emotions and which evoke 'heart-closing' or contracting ones. You might notice your subtle resistance to fully feel your feelings applies as much to your joyful experiences as it does to your painful ones.

Once I received a beautiful card in the post with a loving and grateful message inside. I suddenly had a strong desire to eat and immediately went to the kitchen to find something to nibble on. As soon as I noticed what I was about to do – which would have numbed out my feelings of love and gratitude – I walked back to the windowsill where I'd put the card and read it again, with my hand on my heart, allowing myself to become fully present to the moment, receive the sweetness of the message and let it truly touch me.

All of your feelings and emotions can be felt in your body because they're physical sensations. That's how you can get good at tasting your life with your heart. And being willing to fully feel all your feelings is how you learn to let go of previously unexpressed emotions, unresolved issues and completely free yourself from your past.

VULNERABILITY AND EMOTIONAL CHEMICALS

What's most interesting to me about the cultural fear we have of feeling anything too strong is that trying to *not* feel your feelings (by suppressing, avoiding or ignoring them) is much more troublesome than allowing the 90 second or so intensity of the feeling to wash through you. Suppressing feelings doesn't make them go away. I often have clients who are shocked when they discover how strongly they are feeling about something that happened years or even decades before. It's still there inside them, waiting for their merciful attention.

There can be a lot of shame associated with feelings like jealousy, rage and resentment. But the whole pallet of feelings is universal and felt by everyone. You have access to all of them. You just have to be willing to be open and trust that feeling your feelings won't kill you. Even when grief lasts many years, you allow it all. Emotions need to flow and be released, whenever they arise, preferably, in the moment. Most little children can do this and move through their upset with relative ease. When my son was about five years old he said. "I quite like crying because afterwards you feel smooth."

It might be reassuring to know that, according to the neuroscience, even the most extreme intensity of emotion will last just 90 seconds after the chemicals are released into your system. If the feelings persist longer than that, it's because you are adding your own meaning or story by how you're thinking *about* and interpreting that feeling.

It's much easier to question and change your thoughts and beliefs than your emotions and feelings. Once you are feeling something the chemicals are already in your system. Although you *can* change state mid-flow, it's quite hard to do unless you practice.

If you're interested to learn more about the neuroscience of emotions, check out Jill Bolte Taylor's book, *A Brain Scientist's Personal Journey*. She says, "Once triggered, the chemicals released by my brain surge through my body and I have a physiological experience. Within 90 seconds from the initial trigger, the chemical component of my anger has completely dissipated from my blood and my automatic response is over. If, however, I remain angry after those 90 seconds have passed, then it is because I have chosen to let that circuit continue to run."

For example, it's bad enough that I am upset that you've turned down my invitation to dinner, but if I continue to make added meaning – that you've rejected me, you don't like me, nobody likes me, there's no point in me asking anyone for dinner ever again and I'm going to be all alone for the rest of my life - then I am going to prolong my own agony.

This is why 'going to the balcony' and becoming mindful of your emotional state and listening to your inner dialogue are such powerful practices to develop. You can become adept at making the distinction between your thoughts and feelings. Then you can navigate your way through to what's actually true in any situation, rather than believing your (possibly over-dramatised) assumptions about it. I don't make a distinction between your feelings and emotions - to me they are physical experiences in the body that are universal and can usually be described in a single word. Thoughts are in the mind and are what trigger or feed your feelings and emotions.

What we sometimes list as our 'emotions' are in fact, just thoughts, assumptions and conclusions – like feeling 'ignored'. 'Ignored' isn't actually a feeling. It's a thought - a conclusion you've drawn. The *feeling* you're having is probably disappointment, anger or indignation (another form of anger a bit further down the spectrum). The other person could have their back turned to you and you don't see that they're on the phone, answering an emergency call. The experience of indignation or anger is based on your misinterpretation of the situation. This is a really important distinction to make. Potentially life-saving, quite likely relationship-saving and certainly emotional-life-saving information. I'll say more about this and how it affects your ability to forgive in chapter ten.

Sometimes when people say they 'feel' something (e.g. unlovable), they are often referring to a belief they hold about themselves. It's hard to argue with someone who says they 'feel' unlovable. But 'feeling' unlovable is not really a feeling at all - it's a belief. When you say, "I feel it's true", it just means you believe it. You believe it wholeheartedly. You may have believed it for a very long time. But just because you believe something - that doesn't make it true. And it doesn't become more true over time, if you keep believing it. It's still just a belief. And just because lots of people agree with you about something that doesn't make it true either.

I worked with one client who truly believed she was ugly. At first, she couldn't even think about challenging this childhood belief because it felt too dangerous to question something she'd believed to be fundamentally true about herself for the whole of her life. She said she 'felt' ugly, which was another way of saying she strongly believed it. It didn't mean she *was* ugly. And she really wasn't. It took a lot for her to challenge her own belief, but she faced it and chose to let it go.

VULNERABILITY AND FEAR

Feeling vulnerable, especially when it comes to forgiveness, is all about fear of one kind or another. One example is being afraid that if you forgive someone you might have to go back into relationship with them. I remember a friend challenging me on this, saying they didn't believe I had truly forgiven them because, if I had, I would want to spend time with them again. But actually, my reasons for not wanting to be close friends were still true and valid, even though I was no longer holding onto my resentment. You can choose to forgive and still choose to stay apart.

On the other hand, a defensive, "I don't speak to him any more", position is not the same as forgiveness. Just because you don't see someone any more doesn't necessarily mean you have naturally forgiven them. Out of sight isn't always out of mind. Out of mind doesn't always mean you've resolved the past. Even though time is a great healer, if you don't consciously choose to let go and forgive, the ill will is still likely to be active just a little way under the surface. Your heart will tell you if you are truly at peace, or not, and you can't fake this.

VULNERABILITY, PAIN AND SUFFERING

It's helpful to understand the difference between pain and suffering. Some of the pain in the world is unavoidable. There *is* pain. Shit happens. In fact, you need to know pain so you'll take your hand off a hot stove and don't try to keep walking on a broken leg.

Suffering is your internal rejection of the way things are. The etymology of the word suffering comes from the root 'to carry'. Suffering is the pain that you carry beyond the event itself. It can be measured by the distance between how you want things to be and how they actually are, as well as any extra meaning you assign to that. When you have added meaning, or inaccurately interpreted a situation, you are not only in pain, you're also suffering. It would be bad enough that you experienced abuse, but to then make it mean something negative about who you fundamentally are is just adding insult to the injury.

You are not bad because you have been abused. You are not unlovable because your parents neglected you. You are not stupid because you have made a mistake. You are not evil because you did something that upset someone else and you are not a failure because a plan did not go the way you intended. A project can be a failure. That doesn't mean you are. You can't be - you are always worthy, whole, complete and lovable no matter what. There might be room for improvement in some of your behaviours and choices, but you are always 'a masterpiece in process'. You are always free to question the meaning you have given to a situation, to be kind and encouraging towards yourself and others, and to choose how you respond to life.

VULNERABILITY AND SAFETY

One last reassurance is that even though you can feel vulnerable going through the process of forgiveness, provided that you are not currently in any dangerous situation, forgiveness is completely safe. If you are in a dangerous position, I urge you to get the help and support you need.

Forgiveness is safe for two very important reasons. First, the past is *over*. Whatever it was that happened to you, however traumatic your experience, it's over. That means, with the right therapeutic support, you can heal it. And when you feel strong enough to do your forgiveness work, you can forgive it. You can safely bring the past to the liquid edge of the present and resolve it inside yourself, completely.

Secondly, the realms that you're dealing with are part of the landscape of your own inner world – the thoughts you think, the feelings and emotions you experience, the meanings you make, your worldview, your perspective on life and your values. All of these things, including your imagination, are under your control. You can change and evolve them. Even though forgiveness might feel life threatening, it's actually only holding onto your resentment that's threatening to your emotional and physical wellbeing. That is far more dangerous than forgiveness will ever be.

WELCOMING CHANGE

Just as you need to upgrade your computer software every now and then, so you also need to upgrade and evolve the way you deal with your life. Challenging old beliefs and self-protective behaviour patterns will help you to feel safe enough to forgive. Expanding your capacity to accept the full range of your feelings and allowing yourself to be vulnerable and open to your experience of life is part of that process. Risking being vulnerable can help develop your resilience and the courage to face what you need to in order to forgive.

Forgiveness does require vulnerability, but it undoes emotional knots and blocks in the heart like nothing else. As you become aware of any fear you have around being vulnerable, and learn more in the next chapter about what it is you're really trying to protect, you will be able to make the choice to forgive whenever you feel ready.

Practice Suggestion: Reflect on your relationship with vulnerability. Where does it show up in your life? What makes you feel the most vulnerable? When have you made a choice to protect yourself in the past? When have you 'dared greatly' and taken emotional risks? What happened? What did it require of you to communicate or connect with others in your vulnerability? Make notes in your journal or have a conversation with someone about vulnerability.

CHAPTER FIVE
EGO

"In the morning, when I look at myself in the mirror,
I like to remind myself that I am seeing the person
who is probably going to give me the most trouble that day,
the opponent who will be the biggest obstacle to me
getting what I truly want."

William Ury

A TALE OF TWO SAUSAGES ...cont.

The years passed, and every Christmas dinner was the same. One by one, each member of the family would unwrap their crumpled-up Christmas napkins, lay out the mouldering evidence of their resentments and begin constructing walls between them. Each morsel represented ways they had been let down, hurt, or upset. Each rancid remnant was evidence of how the others had failed to keep their part of the unspoken agreements of conditional family love. Every member of the family was quite certain that if the others had been different, then they would have been happy. They were convinced that the walls were a necessary part of Christmas.

It became a tradition that each family member would bring all their old favourite issues as well as any new grievances against each other in their increasingly large and multiple items of luggage. Year by year, the walls grew so high they could hardly see each other across the table at all. TBC...

EGO

What is it that makes the idea of being vulnerable feel so unbearable? What's really going on here? To understand this knot of resistance to forgiveness, we need to dive into the subtler dynamics of our relationships and what's running them. If you don't understand this piece of the puzzle, it will be hard to forgive anything.

I'm going to use the word 'ego' in a particular way that makes it more relevant to forgiveness. I'm not talking about the Freudian definition of ego as the part of the human psyche that mediates between the id and the superego.

I'm not using ego in the sense of being full of yourself - 'a big ego'. The ego has many responses to the fear of personal vulnerability. It can just as easily play small, disconnect, act passive or submissive, as well as be domineering and aggressive at other times.

The ego, as I'm using the notion, is what we're afraid will get hurt or damaged, or will be exposed and vulnerable, if we forgive. You can't point to that part of you, it's not located anywhere inside your body, it's not a physical structure. But everyone has an ego, and it's usually what you're defending whenever you feel like someone has done something to hurt or upset you that feels hard to forgive.

Your ego is 'the conditioned self'. It's who you think you are - your self-image. It's a composite of all the early programming you received and all the ideals and beliefs (and decisions) you use like scaffolding in the psyche that define who you think you are. Your ego is a conglomeration of everything you think about yourself (both good and bad), the roles you play, the things you're good at, the things you're bad at, your preferences and prejudices, your beliefs and your worldview that make up who you think of as your 'self'.

It's the part of you that feels like it takes the hits of life, when things don't go your way or when other people let you down or don't meet your expectations. The ego can feel contracted, needy, craving and defensive or it can feel aggrandised and entitled.

There isn't really a part of you that's 'crushed' by something someone says, does or doesn't do. Your body will be completely whole and undamaged and your heart still intact and beating steadily. But your ego is a super-sensitive, neurotic creature that is constantly on the look-out for emotional danger and social threats. It needs to know where it should stand and what to do to guarantee its best chance of survival.

The ego takes everything that happens to you personally even when those things aren't actually personal to you at all! You might be upset when it rains on your wedding day. It's not personal, it's just rain. But your ego may make it mean something about life being against you, or it's a bad omen for your marriage, or that you're an unlucky person.

The ego is constantly preoccupied with questions like, "Do I big myself up, here, or should I back down? Should I defend myself or should I avoid confrontation altogether? How can I control this situation? How can I emerge from this looking good? How can I escape from this unscathed?"

I'm not overlooking the beauty of all the positive expressions of your individual, authentic response to life - your creativity, emotions, appreciation, knowledge and love. Each being is unique. We have thoughts, feelings and intuitive capacities, as well as senses, that give us information about the world. The trouble is, all of this data gets passed through the filters of the ego. Ego is what gets in the way of your free-flowing ecstatic engagement with life.

HEARING THE EGO

The ego runs self-protective mechanisms that operate ungoverned, and usually outside of your awareness, until you begin waking up to them. Ego has particular qualities that you can learn to recognise. The easiest way to *hear* the ego is to listen to the voice in your head that is relentlessly commentating on whatever it is you are experiencing. Your ego is usually making a problem out of it too - unless it just liked something in which case it will be desperately trying to keep things exactly as they are. You might not always be aware that you are listening to this voice but its commentary is relentless. It chews over the past and worries about the future. There is one consistent theme, variations of what the Course in Miracles teacher, Earl Purdy, refers to as, "If this were different, I'd be happy".

The major purpose of the ego is to keep you safe under all circumstances. Not just physically safe, but also emotionally safe. It wants to protect you from vulnerability, hurt, humiliation, criticism, stress, feeling any strong emotions and especially from being ordinary - the ego loves to be special. The ego wants to maintain a consistent self-image to the outside world and craves comfort, control and safety.

In *The Untethered Soul,* Michael A Singer says it's as if the ego is saying, "I want everyone to like me. I don't want anyone to speak badly of me. I want everything I say and do to be acceptable and pleasing to everyone. I don't want anyone to hurt me. I don't want anything to happen that I don't like. And I want everything to happen that I do like."

Our early experiences of life lay down the foundational 'programming' that becomes part of who we are. Then we react to the events and experiences of life in specific ways, according to this programming, in an ever-evolving process. Your ego is always updating who you think you are. That includes all the things you like about yourself as well as those things you despair of. It integrates your current experience of life with everything you've learned in the past.

Recent neuroscience research shows your memories are not as fixed as scientists previously thought. Whenever you retrieve a long-term memory it becomes malleable and can be changed in the process. As your brain gets ready to store that recalled memory again, your mind might accidentally or deliberately add extra information (including things that aren't true or weren't part of the original event), so the next time you retrieve the memory, it might include slightly different details.

Perhaps you have a fear of dogs or deep water because of a past experience. The good news is that you can change your memories and behaviour patterns. You can confront your fears, adapt your memory, and learn how to swim or how to pet a dog safely. (Please see the back of the book for resources.)

People are often afraid of public speaking because of past experiences when they've been humiliated or embarrassed in public. Unless you are in physical danger, there is no risk to you in standing in front of a bunch of people and speaking out loud. What's at risk has nothing to do with your physical self and everything to do with your self-image and the exposure of the ego to the possibility that it might be seen by others as not acceptable to them in some way.

If your early circumstances were such that you did better by challenging the status quo or being defensive, your ego will show more of those kinds of traits. If you needed to be a peace-maker and not rock the boat, your ego will primarily operate to protect you by keeping you acting small. There are several systems of personality typing such as the Enneagram which help to identify the different coping mechanisms we develop as we grow.

The ego operates like the filter bubbles in a search engine. The information you search for is biased by all your previous searches. You don't even realise that, most of the time, your experience of life is not what is actually happening at all. It's your unique version of reality, interpreted through the perspective, limited beliefs and layers of meaning made by your ego. We have a cognitive bias called the 'confirmation bias' that favours information that confirms what we already know, rather than anything that challenges it. So, if you *believe* you aren't capable of achieving something, like speaking in public, your mind will tend to find evidence to back up your belief. Just as it will if you believe you can. "Whether you believe you can do a thing or not, you are right." *Henry Ford.*

There's nothing wrong with giving meaning to our experiences per se. We all have to do that to live in the world. We don't want to have to work out what a door is for each time we encounter one. But, sometimes, the assumptions and meanings we assign to things aren't true or beneficial. This can be where many of our inter-personal challenges begin.

The ego is infinitely adaptive. It's a brilliant shape-shifter that will endeavour to keep your continuity-of-self-image programmes running through all circumstances. The voice in your head will argue both sides of a discussion in its tireless efforts to be right. The ego loves the certainty and power that comes with being justified.

The easiest way to *see* the ego in action is in your *behaviour*, particularly when you are under stress. Your reactions to the events of your life are the clues to the underlying, unquestioned beliefs and motives that make up the structure of your ego. If, for example, you learned to be cautious or self-protective in your interactions with others, you will modify your speech, your behaviour and your interpersonal habits to reflect these beliefs. Your inner voice will be guiding you with instructions like; "Don't show your feelings. It's not safe to trust others." etc. When you behave according to the dictates of your ego, you will feel like you're being 'yourself'. This is how your ego ends up running your life and your business.

THE EGO IN RELATIONSHIPS

In James P Carse's book, *Breakfast at the Victory,* he defines ego as, "...the part of the individual that sees itself as above, below or against others."

Ego shows up in your impulse to take offense. It drives the need to judge others to establish where we are in the pecking order - either superior or inferior. It's in that flash of anger when someone has done something you don't like or challenges your ego's self-image. It triggers that self-protective impulse to close your heart when something touches a sore spot. There will be certain subjects that feel 'sacred' to you and other areas that feel taboo. If these get touched on carelessly or in a deliberately harmful way by others, your ego will react by attacking, defending, withdrawing or a combination of responses.

Ego is always driven by fear. Fear of pain, vulnerability, exposure, neglect, missing out, being misunderstood, injustice, the inability to control the behaviour of others and, especially, fear of failure.

Another of its persistent refrains is, "What's wrong with this picture?". The ego's focus is on whatever seems to be lacking, even in the most joyful moments of your life. The ego's voice is dramatic and it completely believes in its own stories. Your ego can also hijack the work of your imagination. The ego uses the filters of its self-interested values, beliefs and behaviours to understand life - not the facts and the verifiable data that's available from the world or other people.

Your ego doesn't just remind you that your relationship has ended, it calls you unlovable and a failure and warns you never to risk falling in love again. It doesn't see the bigger picture or multiple viewpoints, or that you're still a lovable, desirable potential mate for someone else. It only sees its own limited, inaccurate perspective.

MOVING BEYOND THE EGO

Once you become aware of the ego's voice and its tendencies, it's easy to see how much human suffering is created by ego. Most of the suffering you experience is self-inflicted, coming from between your own two ears (or beneath your own umbrella!). The good news is you can transform your relationship to yourself and others by refusing to play the familiar old games as soon as you notice your ego in action.

The moment you recognise you are the one who is hearing the voice of the ego, you have shifted beyond it. You are no longer at one with the voice, you have become the witness to it. You are the observer - the consciousness that can embrace and transcend it. This is the shift you make when you go to the balcony. Once your consciousness has moved beyond ego, to listening to the voice, or observing your behaviour, you can begin to set yourself free from the conditioned self and meet the needs of the moment in a new way.

As Albert Einstein said, "The world as we have created it is a process of our thinking. It cannot be changed without changing our thinking. No problem can be solved from the same level of consciousness that created it."

New opportunities and possibilities will open up in your life and your relationships as you learn to engage with life as it is, without the filters and self-protectiveness of the ego. You move away from blame and being a victim of circumstances and other people, to becoming the conscious author of your attitude and responses to life.

You no longer feel the need to control others or have them be any particular way in order for you to be happy. You stop being defensive and trying to impress people or have them understand you. Can you imagine how freeing it is when you no longer feel you are responsible for trying to control what other people think of you and how everyone else behaves? You might pray the alternative version of the Serenity Prayer:

God grant me the serenity to accept the people I cannot change
The courage to change the one I can
And the wisdom to know that it's me

You genuinely accept other people the way they are. You accept yourself the way you are. You start questioning all of your unconscious beliefs and behaviour patterns and upgrade the ones you want to change.

You still take a stand for what's right, acting for the greatest good in the world, but with an undefended, flexible, responsive heart. When something happens that you don't like or believe shouldn't have happened, you notice this, and you choose how to respond. Your perspective from the balcony gives you a view of other options that might be available to you.

Just a simple action like sending a text can set up an expectation of a particular time-appropriate response. If you're like me, there will be some people in your life you will expect a text back from pretty quickly and others who you won't. If one of the quick responders is a bit slower to respond one day, or doesn't respond at all, you may feel a slight anxiety or discomfort in your body.

When you are more conscious of your ego you will notice this. In David Allen's *Getting Things Done* he talks about 'open loops' which are agreements you've made with yourself or others which are incomplete. These tasks, which still need to be done, subtly pull on your attention until they're resolved. They can be big things or little things, important or trivial, but all take up head space. A text that's left unanswered will stay in the back of your mind until you've had a response. If you pay attention to the voice of your ego, you may be able to hear the extra meaning you've given to why the other person hasn't texted back, "They don't love me anymore, they've died, they've run off with someone else, I don't matter, etc.". You'll be able to feel into the slightly uncomfortable feelings in your body and know that they're a result of your interpretation of the event. This is how you begin to set yourself free from the past and learn to live beyond the confines of your ego.

MEANING MAKING MACHINES

You are always assigning meaning to your experience of life, moment to moment, whether or not you are aware of it. I often refer to this as 'meaning making' and it's very important to understand this mechanism, because of the impact it has on your ability and willingness to forgive.

The realm of the ego is mostly subconscious because of the speed at which your thoughts occur. Many of your habitual responses (especially the ones you deplore) will be automatic until you notice them and can then choose to do something about them. This is the same for everyone. A lot of the reason why we struggle with other people's unconscious behaviour is because it reminds us of our own. When you pay attention to your thoughts, with the intention to hear the voice of your ego, it's like opening a drop-down menu bar on your computer screen. When you click on the title, you can see all the other information you weren't aware of before listed underneath.

The best tool I know for dealing effectively with how your mind makes up meaning, and cutting through the ego's fearful mis-representation of reality, is to question that inner dialogue or 'mindtalk'. I'll cover this tool in more depth in chapter ten. (Please also see resources section at the back of the book.)

My practice is to write down everything that's bothering me - an uncensored list of the diatribe in my mind. I then ask myself, "Is this thought true, false or something I don't know". It's the fastest and most effective way I know to free myself from the grip of my ego. This is because I am exposing my ego to the light, and it loves to dwell unquestioned in the shadowy depths of half-truths and shocking possibilities. This is how you shift your perspective out of a limited, biased, conditioned ego stance to a more aware, objective, higher view from the balcony. It's like panning for the gold of truth.

Once you've discerned which of the statements you wrote down are true (quite possibly very few or none at all) you can replace the doom-mongering or fantasies of your ego with the facts of the situation and make clear, powerful choices based on that truth.

This isn't like using positive affirmations such as "I am rich" when you're struggling to pay your rent. Or using turnarounds, where rather than saying "He is selfish", you turn the sentence around and say, "He is *not* selfish" or "*I* am selfish" instead. These aren't the right techniques if you're trying to get to the objective truth of the matter. You're not trying to deny what happened, either. You're not saying, "My parents were paragons of virtue", when you were abused, abandoned or disinherited. You're making a statement of fact e.g. "Sometimes he behaves selfishly", with no additional meaning tacked on at all.

THE EGO AND YOUR FEELINGS

The ego is afraid of your feelings. It tries to control everything so you don't have to feel. Its primary objective is to keep you free of all pain. But it's natural to feel regret and remorse and to grieve the past, when you've experienced challenging events. If feelings arise the best thing to do is feel them in the moment. Otherwise they'll just wait to come back at a later, and potentially less convenient, time. Make room for your feelings. Let the waves rise and fall. Once the intensity of the feeling has subsided, you can enquire into whether or not there was any ego-story attached. But in the fullness of the moment – just feel.

When you do something differently, like questioning the meaning you are assigning to your story, it will feel unfamiliar and maybe a little uncomfortable. This is a good sign - something to welcome rather than avoid - because it means you are changing. Your ability to tolerate that discomfort will serve you because you will be breaking your familiar patterns of thinking and behaving in the process. You'll also be developing a valuable capacity to feel deeply and not be overwhelmed or distressed by the strength of your feelings.

As you learn to let yourself feel your emotions more deeply as they pass through your system, you will find they naturally resolve. You will have fewer and fewer experiences that you fear and you will develop inner resilience, through facing into your pain as well as expanding your capacity for greater happiness and joy.

THE EGO AND YOUR HAPPINESS

It's only your ego that feels afraid to let go of the past and truly forgive. Sometimes it's hard to let go of wishing things had been different. But coming to terms with what happened, and accepting it, is the beginning of forgiveness and how you find true peace of mind.

It's also a mighty relief to give up wishing people would stop doing the things that upset, annoy or trigger you and to stop wishing they'd change or apologise. When you forgive, you free yourself from making your happiness depend on what another person does or doesn't do. It still doesn't mean you condone unacceptable behaviour. Just that you claim back responsibility for your own happiness and ask for what you need. If the other person can't or won't give it, you don't have to bear a grudge or blame them, you can just ask elsewhere. You choose what requests you make of another person and whether or not you stay in relationship with them.

I think of the relationship dynamic this way: imagine there is a gate between you and the other person. On one side is your land, on the other side is their land. You are 100% responsible for everything that happens up to the gate. Your thoughts, your feelings, your behaviour, your choices. The gate is where you meet and beyond the gate is 100% *their* responsibility. It's the same with life. There is a point beyond which you have no control over what happens to you.

You only have control over your attitude and response on your side of the gate.

It's even more of a relief to be able to apply the same principles to the past. Your ego will have played its part in the stories you've told yourself about your life - including adding meaning to events that may or may not be true. You are 100% responsible for how you remember your past. Even though the ego loves to dwell on the past and is afraid of the future, you can choose to free yourself from your past pain and create an inspiring new future for yourself instead.

FORGIVENESS AND TRUE POWER

If there is something going on between you and another person that is abusive, then you need to take steps to address it. Even when forgiveness has become your way of life, you will need to take action, take a stand for what's true and call for changes that need to be made. You can still press charges, or seek restorative justice, without bearing resentment or coming from your ego.

I was once in a difficult phase of a relationship where the other person would verbally insult me during unavoidable phone calls. I'd tell them I would be willing to speak to them at another time, when they were able to speak civilly. Then I'd hang up the call. I'd listen to my inner dialogue, and notice what I was believing in that moment (e.g. "This person doesn't care about me", "My needs don't matter", "I have to fight to get my needs met"). Then I'd go through each piece of my mindtalk and ask myself, "Is this limiting belief (about this situation and this person) true, false or something I don't know?" Once I could discern what was actually true, I'd make a new choice, based on that truth. If there was something within my power that I could do differently, I'd do that. I also did my forgiveness work. I refused to hold any ill will against that person and that situation. Now, years later, I'm friends with this person and they have had a significant role in my life.

FORGIVENESS, VULNERABILITY AND RESENTMENT

So how does all of this tie together? How will forgiveness serve your ego? Most likely, it won't. Your ego will only want you to forgive if you stand to gain something from it. The ego's efforts will mostly be to try and remove you from any risk of being vulnerable. It will close ranks around your heart and shut off the emotional blood supply to stop you from feeling any hurt, vulnerability or pain. The unfortunate side effect of this is it also stops you from feeling full-on joy, gratitude, pleasure, ecstasy and love. All you're left with is the numbness of your shut-down heart.

Your ego will not want to stand down if there is a way you can claim the moral high ground and protect, absolve and defend yourself. Your ego will also avoid making significant decisions, excuse your behaviour, and play victim or martyr if it thinks that will serve you.

The ego will want to be self-righteous or just *right* for once - then it might be interested in forgiveness. Depending on the circumstances, the ego will present whatever face will get it the best results. It will combine multiple perspectives in a spectacular effort to absolve you of any responsibility in your relationship problems and pile every ounce of blame onto the other person.

The combination of all of these obstacles make forgiveness seem like the last thing anyone would do, but once you see how all of these different aspects of resistance to forgiving play out, you will also see how the ego's defences are really just a house of cards - your ego can't really protect you from anything at all. We're all vulnerable, we all experience loss, pain, misunderstanding and we all have an ego. What you're trying to defend by not forgiving is an illusion.

Authentic forgiveness is the absolute refusal to hold ill will and to not condemn or write off someone because of what they did or didn't do. You give up the ill will, you surrender it, even though the ego is afraid of the vulnerability of surrender. The kind of patronising,

"You are so wrong and bad, yet I, from my lofty heights, have deigned to bestow forgiveness upon your reprehensible head" is not authentic forgiveness. That is the ego's version of forgiveness.

Forgiveness is not the abandonment of all morality and values. We take a stand against abuse, violence, rape and all violations of human rights. But *not forgiving,* and holding ill will, won't add one ounce of strength or power to your efforts. It only adds to your ego. It doesn't matter how much resentment or ill will you carry, or how many years or decades you've carried it for, it won't change or resolve the past. Your resentment can't change the other person. And only clear, powerful, effective, enlightened action will change the future.

Change only happens when you act. The clearer you are about your motivations for acting, and the less ego-driven mindtalk you have about the situation, then the easier it will be for you to find a powerful and effective response that serves the greatest good of all concerned.

As you become more aware of all the games the ego plays, this will also help to make you more compassionate and less easily deceived by other people's egos. Free of the filters of your ego, you can decide from a much clearer place what choice needs to be made in response to your circumstances.

THE EGO AND RESENTMENT

Being aware of your ego's games is critical in making forgiveness easy, because once you understand what your ego is up to, you can see how your ego uses resentment like a multi-purpose super-tool.

The last piece in the puzzle to understand why we resist forgiveness so wholeheartedly, is resentment itself. From the ego's perspective, resentment seems to have many advantages and no disadvantages. But, in the next chapter, I'll show you how the resentment you're carrying is fatally toxic to you and everyone you have a relationship with. It's like chemotherapy that uses "nonspecific intracellular poisons" that don't just kill the cancer cells, but impact your entire immune system. Resentment poisons your whole life.

Practice Suggestion: *Start noticing your ego. Notice its voice, its fears, its behaviours and habits. See if you can notice the feeling of contraction that most often accompanies it, or the feeling of defensiveness, or righteousness. What circumstances are more likely to bring your ego out to the fore? What are your ego's favourite refrains and complaints? What makes your ego happy? Conversely, when do you notice you are relatively free of ego – when are you in your flow state, authentic, positive, productive, creative and peaceful?*

CHAPTER SIX
RESENTMENT

*"Holding on to anger and resentment is like
setting yourself on fire and hoping the other person
will be bothered by the smoke."*

Anon

A TALE OF TWO SAUSAGES ...cont.

*This year, the mother had invited a special, wise guest for Christmas
dinner. Everyone gathered round the beautifully set table and
emptied their suitcases full of grievances onto the pretty red
tablecloth. The pile of hardened, withered sausages and rancid
resentments was so high it covered the decorations and the place
settings and spilt over onto the floor. There was no room for the
Christmas turkey or even a single candlestick anywhere on the table.*

*The only person who didn't put any mouldy old foodstuff on the table
was the wise woman. She was busy rummaging in her tiny bag. The
family stood up from their seats to peek over the piles of resentments,
curious to see what she would add to the table. But the wise woman
just pulled out an old-fashioned wooden clothes peg and applied it
firmly to her nose.*

*After they'd all put their hands to their hearts and given thanks for
the meal, the wise woman said, in a slightly nasal tone, "I'm*

fascinated by your most unusual family tradition. I've spent time with lots of different families, but I've never seen such an extensive collection of mouldy sausages. How did this all begin?"

The wise woman made a sweeping gesture with her left hand and, instantly, the whole family except the eldest daughter fell into a deep sleep-like trance.

"Well," said the eldest daughter, taking a deep breath, "Let me tell you all about it…." TBC…

RESENTMENT

The etymology of the word resentment comes from the Latin 'sentir' – to feel. Re-*sent*-ment – literally means 'to feel again'. Resentment is feeling all the feelings associated with a situation / person / event / trauma over and over again. You *re-send* those same old feelings around your system every time you remember the trigger event or the circumstances, however many years ago it happened. This sets up an infinite loop of resentment that you can never get out of unless you do something to resolve the situation.

Resentment is implicated in every conflict, divorce, falling out with a friend or family member. Ultimately, what it boils down to is that one party didn't do what the other wanted or expected them to. Always it's the ego insisting "If you were different, I'd be happy".

The perceived misdemeanour is noted, followed by the harbouring and hardening of anger into resentment and, finally, the (seeming) inability to let it go. All of this happens unconsciously inside you, until you become aware that you don't feel as loving as you used to or that you're acting out in other ways, and the war has begun. Every unmet expectation has the potential to become a future resentment.

We have previously written scripts for all the players in our lives and, most of the time, they haven't even read the script, let alone learned their lines properly or know when their cues are! Other people say the wrong things, do the wrong things, forget the wrong things, turn up late or early, don't buy the thing you wanted, or buy something else you hate, they laugh in the wrong places, let you down, show you up, don't understand what's most important to you and unwittingly say things that feel hurtful – in minor and more significant ways.

Resentment seems to have a magnetic potency to it. When you resent someone for one thing, it's easy to find other reasons to resent them too. Under your tab for that person you may have a very long drop-down list of grievances, especially if you've known each other for a while.

This is why most relationships begin to deteriorate, because we are gathering little sausages of grudges and grievances against each other. The list may get spilt out as a tsunami of grievance during an argument, but most of the time you'll just keep the misdemeanours to yourself and build up a wall around your heart.

It's not just intimate or family relationships where resentment accumulates. It's every relationship we have – with colleagues, friends, organisations and people we've never even met. That list includes ourselves. Often the hardest person to forgive is ourselves and I'll say more about that in later chapters.

Resentment usually feels less hot than the original anger - as if the feeling has cooled and solidified over time into what the book, *A Course in Miracles,* calls a "dark shield of grievance". Hot, cold or otherwise, however you are feeling it, the poison is in *your* system – not the other person's. Forgiveness is the one and only antidote to the poison of resentment. These are your choices:

- Take appropriate action to seek amends, if that's possible
- Let go of your resentment and forgive
- Both of the above

Forgiveness does not exclude restorative justice, seeking compensation or making amends. Forgiveness is the *letting go of the ill* will held over time.

FOR GOOD REASON

Even if you're mistaken in your interpretation of events, you will be carrying your resentment for *some* reason. Brad Brown's definition of resentment is, *"Ill will held over time against someone or something for 'good reason'"*.

This is helpful in several ways. Firstly, it acknowledges that sometimes you really *are* hurt by the things others do or don't do. I have worked with many clients who, most commonly as children, were the victims of abuse, violence and neglect. All of them had really 'good reasons' for resenting their abusers.

'For good reason' is obviously going to be relative. To some, a particular incident will be outrageous and unacceptable. To another, it might just be seen as a regrettable mistake. Sometimes even a relatively mild incident of bullying, or being called an unkind or untrue name, can have a devastating effect on someone. It can be as impactful and significant as the effect of much more serious abuse on someone else.

What's important is that there's an acknowledgement that something actually *did* happen - even if you have a different version of the story from the perpetrator. If you've been raped, abused or injured it probably isn't helpful to you to hear spiritual platitudes like, 'everything's perfect the way it is' or that you 'asked' for this experience because there are karmic lessons to be learned. Some spiritual teachings can be interpreted to mean that since, ultimately, nothing has happened and nothing really exists so there's nothing to forgive at the level of spirit. However, I suggest that you start in the physical and emotional realms and acknowledge the reality of what you experienced and its consequences. Events in life affect us and continue to do so until we are ready to resolve the past and forgive what needs to be forgiven. In order to truly let go of the past you will need to feel all your feelings about what happened - especially if you repressed them or didn't know how to deal with them at the time.

It takes enormous courage to face the raw pain of abuse, neglect, betrayal or trauma. It's natural to have an aversion to 'opening a can of worms' and to want to forget about the past instead. The trouble is, it doesn't matter how far down you bury it, like radioactive waste, it doesn't stop being active just because you've encased it in concrete. Concrete can crack. The only way to resolve it is to face it.

Secondly, the 'good reason' part of holding onto resentment also points to the advantages the ego will be gaining from not letting it go. There are a number of ways the ego seems to benefit from holding onto resentment. I'll cover those next but, as an example, resentment might feel like it's protective in some way, and you'd feel powerless and too vulnerable without it. To the self-protective mechanisms of the ego, holding on to your resentment might *feel* safer than the alternative of letting go of it, but there are enormous hidden costs to this choice.

Even when you can justify your resentment, there are potential pitfalls to believing you have 'good' reason for resenting someone. There's always the chance you have jumped to a conclusion that wasn't true or that you've misunderstood something about the situation. Our memories are notoriously unreliable, even about 'facts'. Your ego's version of events may paint you as an innocent bystander, when you may have had some responsibility for what happened.

HELD OVER TIME

'Held over time' can also be relative. It's quite possible to feel resentful immediately after an event occurs, but it's more likely that your initial response will be anger.

Resentment can accumulate over time especially when you don't express your upset when something happens. If the other person denies or justifies what they did in a way that dismisses, or refuses to accept, your objection to their behaviour you could be left with a feeling that the issue is unresolved and carry your resentment about it from then on. If you back down in the face of someone else's anger and don't say what needed to be said, the same thing can happen. Anger can be a drive to take action, so if you ignore it, suppress it and don't deal with what happened either with the other person, or in yourself, the likely long-term consequence will be resentment - both of the person concerned and of yourself for not speaking up.

Over time your anger may feel less active. This is especially true if you have been good at finding ways to numb out your emotions. Your anger will sink below the surface of your awareness and crust over as resentment. Other emotions like jealousy and envy can also convert into resentment in a similar way.

ADMITTING IT

You might feel a bit reluctant to admit you're harbouring ill will towards another person or thing. Wishing harm, misfortune or unhappiness on another person is part of the instinct for revenge.

I definitely felt resistance, embarrassment and shame when I first made a resentment list during a personal development weekend workshop devised by Brad Brown and W Roy Whitten (the More to Life programme – see the resources section of the book for more details). We were invited to write down a list of all the people we held some kind of grievance against, or judged or held in disdain. We were also encouraged to add in our resentment of 'things' as well – like the government, or the weather or our weight.

I could feel a subtle closing of my heart as my egoic indignation rose up against people who'd treated me badly and I remembered upsetting circumstances from the past. I decided to lower my bar for defining what I'd count as resentment to include tiny grudges, grievances and judgements as well as all the bigger, more 'justifiable' indignation and anger I was holding on to.

I realised that in some small way or another I probably resented pretty much everyone I'd ever met plus a lot of people I never had! I didn't think of myself as a particularly resentful person, (and my ego still doesn't) but I wanted to be thorough.

When I felt into my heart, I noticed I mildly resented friends who were more successful or talented or had more resources than me. I resented ex-lovers who had hurt me, co-workers, bosses, family members, the weather, more successful but flaky musicians and people who drove too fast, especially on my side of the road. I resented old friends I wasn't in touch with anymore and some I still saw, old boyfriends even though I hadn't been interested in them for years, the priest at the church I went to as a girl, people who were irresponsible, businesses that trashed the environment and so on.

I started my list, got on a roll, and around number 36 I thought, "Yes, I probably resent my mother as well," and wrote her name down too. Later on, I realised that my resentment of my mother was far deeper than I had imagined and was having consequences in many areas of my life that I hadn't, until then, been able to see.

One of my reasons for being hesitant about admitting that I held any resentment against my mother was because of her illness. She'd been suffering from multiple sclerosis for many years and by the time I was fifteen years old her increasing debilitation was starting to have a profound impact on our family.

By my eighteenth birthday, I was pushing her in her wheelchair around the block to get her hair done by a lady who had a disabled access hairdressing salon. By the time I was twenty, I was cooking for her, helping to feed her, clean her and lift her on and off the toilet many times a day. I took my third year off from my university degree to live at home with her, my brother and my dad, because no-one was coping with her increasing disabilities.

It might seem mean to resent someone for something that's beyond their control, but that was what I finally admitted to myself. I resented my mother for being ill and for the impact that it had on me and our family.

D.E.N.I.A.L. (Don't Even (K)now I Am Lying)

I think it's pretty normal to not notice, or be unwilling to admit, you're holding onto resentment. You'll usually be focussed on how wrong the other person is rather than on your own ill will. But you also might not recognise what you're feeling *is* resentment, especially when the anger has 'gone cold'. You might just feel numb, closed down, or like you're 'over it', especially if you no longer have any contact with that person. Or you could be in denial that there is anything that still needs to be addressed, felt or let go of.

To those of us who consider ourselves kind-hearted, reasonable, emotionally intelligent or even spiritually aware people, the idea of admitting our resentment can seem distasteful or embarrassing or too 'negative'. But my guess is that, unless you are actively engaging with forgiveness, you're probably still running *some* resentment somewhere in your life! I was at a spiritual conference in London once, and heard one of the participants complaining to the organisers that she was so angry with someone at her table that she wanted to hit her! Spiritual ego is still ego (in floatier clothing!).

I sometimes work with clients who say things like, "Oh no, I don't *resent* them. I'm just disappointed" or "I'm a little bit cross about it."

To me, that always qualifies. Feeling anger, upset, 'tired of', judgemental, critical or negative are all clues that you may be about to gather another sausage for your resentment pile. Point-scoring, taking offence, feeling hurt about, unkindness, blaming, condemnation and being dismissive are all forms of mild resentment too. Resentment and anger are on a spectrum of emotions that range in intensity from mild irritation and annoyance to intense fury and incandescent rage.

In certain relationships, you might be able to see the good points about someone which outweigh the things that drive you crazy, but nevertheless, still feel some subtle resentment. This will only show up every now and then if you get triggered by something that hits one of your sacred taboos or sensitive spots.

Some of my clients have been reluctant to admit feeling resentment against someone, like a parent who had died, because they've worried it would seem disloyal to their memory. These clients would admit to feeling guilty for speaking, or even thinking, badly of their parent or relative. This was true even if they had been the victim of abuse. Relationships can be complex. We can simultaneously acknowledge the positive elements in the connection, the sacrifices that were made, and be compassionate about the other person's circumstances, while also recognising that some behaviour towards us was abusive.

Admitting your resentment is not dishonouring of someone. It's just being truthful about what happened, what's going on inside you now, and giving yourself full permission to embrace it. Once you've admitted to yourself that you're carrying resentment, you know your next step is to do your forgiveness work.

I really didn't want to admit that I resented my mother for being ill because she didn't have any choice about it and I was ashamed of being mean and cold-hearted. During that weekend training, we were invited to do a forgiveness process on one of the people on our list. I chose to do my forgiveness process on my mother. I experienced enormous relief once I let go of all the resentment I was holding against her and forgave her for everything, especially her illness. Later on, I also forgave myself for having resented her, too.

After I had done my forgiveness work I visited her in the nursing home where she lived for the last eight years of her life. I felt so much more compassionate, open-hearted and loving than I had done in all the previous years of her illness. Even though she wasn't able to recognize who I was, it felt like something had healed between us.

Since that time, I have done several more processes, forgiving my mother and our very challenging circumstances at a deeper and deeper level each time. My most recent process was about asking her for forgiveness for my own emotional shut-down and the ways I treated her - sometimes being irritable, snappy and withdrawn. I also took the time, again, to forgive myself for how I'd behaved.

This is subtle territory and your ego may be reluctant to engage with forgiveness unless you reassure it that it's safe and there's more to be gained by forgiving than holding on to your resentment. We'll go more deeply into that in the next chapter.

BINDWEED AND DANDELIONS

Resentment can be like bindweed – a very fast-growing garden weed that winds itself around other plants, eventually choking them completely. Sometimes resentment isn't obvious because it's hidden by indifference or ambivalence towards someone. This is especially likely to be true with your parents. Often there's a lot to be grateful for, but, even if all you're grateful to them for is your existence, the bindweed of resentment may be threaded through your appreciation.

As you grow up, you might be able to appreciate that your parents were probably doing the best they could at the time. However, they might not have been. They might have been downright selfish, irrational, narcissistic, addicted, cruel or abusive. You might be able to rationalise and accept some of their behaviour, but you are likely to also need to forgive them for what they did or didn't do. Even if you have done some personal /spiritual development work along the way, and given yourself the time and space to process your past, if you haven't actually forgiven them, it still needs to be done.

Some of your resentment may be relatively easy to find and pull up. Some might be like bindweed with perennial regenerative root systems and some other might be really difficult to dig out because it has deep tap roots like dandelions.

Sometimes, resentment can be about something that happened a long time ago that's hard to let go of. It may have been a relatively small incident, but as a consequence, you made some decisions about who you are and what might be possible for you that have affected the rest of your life. There are many stories where a child is told they can't do something by an adult, or someone they respect or trust, and then they completely shut down on a favourite hobby like singing or writing.

It's easy to make the mistake of dwelling on what happened, rather than notice what the weeds of your resentment are keeping choked up in you.

Jack Canfield, who co-wrote *Chicken Soup for the Soul,* tells the story of Catherine Lanigan who, as an undergraduate, was given advice by one of her tutors that she shouldn't write or even think of herself as a writer. Seventeen years later, a screenwriter challenged her on that belief and offered her an opportunity to write. She took the challenge and went on to write almost forty published titles including *Romancing the Stone* and *The Jewel of the Nile* – both of which were also made into movies.

Maybe you are aware of a time in your own life when you made an unconscious decision to protect yourself, but this then became a limiting belief, and eventually a habit, that is still having a detrimental effect on your life today? It will take a conscious decision to undo the old programming that is still operating in you. Most of us have old patterns of behaviour that need to be uninstalled and replaced by upgraded software - new beliefs and behaviours.

RESENTMENT AS A WAY OF LIFE

As my mother used to say before her illness, "Just because everybody's doing it, doesn't make it right." Just because carrying resentment is ubiquitous, doesn't mean it's beneficial to anyone.

There seems to be an unspoken cultural agreement that resentment is normal, understandable, justifiable and even recommended. Don't let them get away with it! Don't get mad, get even! Think about all the soaps, movies and literature where revenge is at the heart of the plot (and of course there are a few movies and shows with forgiveness as the theme - just not so many.) It's easy to persuade other people to agree that your resentment is justified, especially when you have 'good reasons'. According to Michael E McCulloch's research in *Beyond Revenge – the Evolution of the Forgiveness Instinct*, the impulse for revenge has always been part of our biological evolutionary inheritance. He also suggests that wherever there are effective systems of justice, we no longer need to seek vengeance in barbaric ways. Even though the law will only go so far in redressing wrongs, vengeance isn't the answer, no matter who agrees with you.

Everyone is subject to the 'bandwagon effect' – the tendency to believe or do things that other people do. It's just another of the cognitive biases. We're much more likely to eat a dessert when we're dining out with friends who are also having dessert. And we're more likely to help ourselves to a large portion of the yummy cheesecake of group resentment - even if we're only resenting people who don't forgive or don't eat cheesecake! But much like real cheesecake, there are consequences to consuming it in large quantities and I will go into those in the next chapter.

I remember a situation in one family where a mother was carrying resentment, on behalf of her daughter, against another family member and had stopped communicating with them. Second-hand resentment, a hand-me-down passed from family member to family member or from generation to generation, is horribly common. This is how you get to sustain a hundred-year war.

THE JOYS OF RESENTMENT

Resentment is like superfuel for the ego. The ego trades in resentment and uses it like a multi-purpose fluid. Resentment can also bond you with others who have the same prejudices or world view. Thinking about revenge and getting even activates the part of the brain known as the 'reward system'. However, resentment has serious side effects and can slowly poison your whole life. It comes at an exorbitant price that most of us aren't aware we're paying.

As Brené Brown says of resentment, "It might go down like a milkshake, but it burns up your insides like battery acid." Even though it's poisonous, there are a number of subtle 'payoffs', or benefits, to the ego for holding on to the deliciously deadly cocktail of resentment, self-righteous anger and blame. We must be getting *something* out of not letting our grievances go, otherwise we wouldn't do it.

When I gently suggest this idea to a client, I'm often met with a "Nope, I'm not getting anything out of it at all". This is completely normal. You have to be brutally honest with yourself and willing to face your ego in order to really see the subtle games you're playing and do something about it.

The best way to approach this exploration into the joy of resentment is with an open mind, curiosity and a touch of humour.

You may even feel a little uncomfortable. See that as a good thing – you're going to discover what your ego's been up to!

THE SOFA-CUSHION OF RESENTMENT

Sometimes, when I work with a client, I put an enormous sofa cushion on their laps to represent the size and weight of their resentment so they can experience physically what they're carrying by holding onto it. They immediately feel safe and protected behind the thick sofa-cushion wall. They understand how their resentment helps to create and maintain emotional distance between them and the person they're resenting.

They also feel shocked by the weight of the gigantic burden they're now aware they've been carrying around. The pain they are feeling is still there but now it's stuffed behind the sofa cushion. The past has still happened, the events occurred, the pain is unchanged. They often also become more aware of the feelings and words that didn't get expressed at the time, that are now suffocated under the enormous cushion.

When the payoff for holding on to resentment is a feeling of safety - no matter how false - it can feel *dangerous* to your psyche to even consider the idea of letting it go. It feels way too vulnerable.

THE ULTIMATE PROTECTOR

Protection is probably the most common use of resentment. This is how I was using it - to protect me from the pain of being a young carer and the daughter of a mother who wasn't able to function in the same way as my friends' mothers. It felt easier to close down my heart and wall it off behind a shield of resentment than to feel the pain of circumstances that were completely beyond my control. I used to (passive-aggressively) wear a badge that declared "Je ne regrette rien" and prided myself on the fact that I didn't cry for seven years.

Resentment works like a circuit breaker. The intense feelings are buffered and not fully felt or expressed. It's natural to want to avoid feeling bad. Everything in your physiology is programmed to help you avoid pain and seek pleasure. But there are massive downsides to using resentment to *avoid* feeling your feelings. No-one *wants* to feel pain. But if you don't let yourself feel the pain, loss, disappointment or hurt around someone or certain circumstances, these feelings can never be resolved. You will also be living with the stress of unexpressed emotions that keep wanting to surface. You might find yourself feeling tearful (at unrelated times) or depressed or aware that you're finding ways to avoid the unresolved issue.

AVOIDING SIGNIFICANT DECISIONS

We are programmed by our biological evolutionary drives to connect and bond, and some people believe any kind of relationship is better than none. When you hold on to your resentment you can also end up holding on to a dysfunctional relationship rather than letting both go. It can feel safer to keep on complaining, resenting and blaming someone else, whilst maintaining an emotionally distant relationship, rather than take responsibility for your part in what's not working and initiate uncomfortable change. This might mean the end of the relationship altogether. Resentment can feel like a connection, even when the relationship is over and you know you need to move on.

In the workplace it might feel easier to moan and put up with a toxic boss or colleague than to call them on their behaviour, rock the boat and risk losing your job. You can end up avoiding making significant life decisions out of fear of change and use your resentment to justify your choice.

NUMBING THE PAIN OF COMPASSION

Self-tenderness and compassion can also be feelings we'd prefer to avoid or numb ourselves from. Pity is the natural feeling of tenderness that is evoked by any distress or misfortune, along with the desire for its relief - for ourselves and for others. But we can be especially resistant to the idea of opening our hearts to *ourselves*. It's related to our fear of vulnerability and our reluctance to feel anything too deeply – positive or negative. We're afraid that if we're too gentle and tender with ourselves we might never get ourselves back together again. We might have learned that it wasn't acceptable to 'wallow in self-pity'.

You may be afraid that if you open your heart to yourself you'll have to open your heart to everyone else, including the person you're resenting. That may feel too vulnerable. You may also be afraid that if you feel compassion for the other person, it will ruin your resentment story and you will be exposed or weak without it.

Interestingly, according to the latest neuroscience, feeling pity for others is good for your mind and brain and feeling pity for yourself is even better.

There's an important difference between blaming and resenting yourself for something you've done and taking full responsibility for your action, while staying compassionate towards yourself. Being accountable for your actions is taking full responsibility for your choices, with your heart open. Blame is only about who is at fault. Heart closed. As William Ury says, "Self-understanding without self-responsibility runs the risk of dissolving into self-pity. Self-responsibility without self-understanding can deteriorate into self-blame. To get to yes with yourself, you need both."

THE ALLURE / MIS-USE OF SELF PITY

In excess, self-pity can also be a hidden *payoff* for holding on to resentment. You might not want to admit it, but there may be subtle ways in which you use your story to believe or excuse certain things about yourself. You might justify certain behaviour or treat yourself in a particular way, e.g. if you tell yourself you're a hopeless failure, you might not even let yourself begin a creative project you've wanted to do all your life. You might use your self-pity to get something or deny something from others, or you might mis-use your self-pity to justify being unhealthily self-indulgent. There's an important distinction between self-compassion and tenderness, and seeing yourself as a hopeless case. When you feel compassionate and tender-hearted, you are treasuring yourself, not condemning yourself to a victim position.

THE SHADOW OF BEING A VICTIM

The word 'victim' can be contentious and another minefield of misunderstanding. Surely, there are no advantages to being a victim? We are victims to the extent that things happen to us that are beyond our control. And a lot happens beyond our control. Most of life's big events happen *to* us, starting with being born, which is why the ego is so desperate to maintain some semblance of control. When you believe you are a victim, or have truly been victimised (because circumstances were beyond your control), the act of holding on to resentment can feel like you've claimed back some power or control, even though that's not actually possible.

Human beings need to make sense of their reality, especially as children. So if like me, one of your parents is repeatedly chiding you for being stupid, you will start to believe that it's true. It will become part of your ego identification and you'll adopt behaviours that try to counter this limiting belief like studying hard or needing to know everything to avoid being seen as stupid. Alternatively, you might not even try to achieve anything or fulfil your potential because you are afraid of making mistakes, or believe that you don't have much to offer.

Using resentment to maintain your victimhood can give you licence to avoid taking responsibility for the parts of your life that you *do* have control over. Holding on to your resentment is a way of keeping that story alive in yourself. You might justify choosing softer options and avoid the risk of showing up powerfully in the world. In this case, it's holding on to your resentment that's disempowering you and not the events that happened.

It's like someone runs over your favourite teddy bear and then you carry the squashed toy around with you for the rest of your life. If someone harmed you in the past, and you don't let go of your resentment, you're allowing them to harm you again every single day. You're also reinforcing the neural pathways in your brain that maintain that story about you and its associated behaviours.

If you start to *identify* yourself as a victim there's a danger it will become part of your self-image. You are more than the circumstances of your life. You don't have to live your life as a victim of them, even though you may have suffered from events that were beyond your control. Yes, you may have been a victim at one time in your life, but you are not fundamentally a victim of life.

If you continue to identify yourself as a victim, you might never step back far enough from your story, to see the limiting beliefs you're holding about yourself or to question them. You always have a choice whether or not to believe your mindtalk and any limiting beliefs that say you are unlovable or unworthy because of what happened to you. You don't have to be a victim of your own resentment, either. You can choose how far you carry your ill will down the path of your life.

One of my clients endured a horrific childhood of neglect, abuse and deprivation, but she no longer thinks of herself as a victim of her circumstances. She's done a lot of forgiveness work on her family of origin and now if you ask her, she says "I have no complaints about my childhood." She is a testament to what's possible through forgiveness and therapeutic support.

THE POWER OF MARTYRDOM

You could also be subtly using your resentment to keep yourself identified with the role of martyr. This dynamic can show up in any relationship. The year I took off college to take care of my family because of my mother's deteriorating health was definitely a 'martyr' year for me. By holding on to my resentment of my mother's illness, I could identify myself as a compassionate martyr and justify taking advantage of the situation in various ways. I accepted money from my father, feeling like my parents 'owed' me because of the sacrifice I'd made. I also won a lot of 'martyr points' with my family and friends, particularly the Catholic ones. Everyone thought I was a wonderful daughter and thought highly of my service to my family.

What I was really doing was avoiding my teaching practice year because I wasn't sure I even wanted to be a teacher given my resentment of the education system itself. Being a martyr for a year nicely absolved me of the responsibility of making a choice to quit college, change degree or attempt to alter the whole education system. I was too busy being a martyr!

THE POWER OF SELF-RIGHTEOUSNESS
(How High Is My Horse Exactly?)

An additional bonus to carrying victim or martyr flavours of resentment is the delicious payoff of self-righteousness. The ego so loves to be right. Self-righteousness is the ultimate justification for holding on to resentment. The steps up to the highest horses are made entirely of resentment!

Sometimes there's a kind of righteous anger that demands action. Like speaking out against injustice or standing up for some kind of change that would serve the world. If a situation has been building up for a while, it's possible to use the energy of anger as a 'final straw' to make a necessary change. But the trouble is, when action is driven out of resentment, it's reactive behaviour. Reactive behaviour is automatic and unconscious, whereas *responding* to a situation is considered and conscious. This includes taking the highest, widest, most objective view from the balcony, and acting for the greatest good for all concerned.

The other danger with self-righteously driven resentment is that it can become the justification for all kinds of unconscious and destructive behaviour. This can range from not taking good care of yourself, being rude or obnoxious, to cutting someone out of your life completely, having an affair, abusing alcohol or drugs and inflicting harm on others.

This is how any kind of fundamentalism works. You claim the moral high ground because other people are not adhering to the same moral/political/religious values as you. You feel you have the right to treat some people badly or differently from how you treat others, whilst seeing yourself as justified, innocent and self-righteous. Peering down from your very high horse those others will seem lowly by comparison.

If you've been treated badly by someone, your ego might score some self-righteousness points for you by thinking, "Well, at least I'm not as bad as *they* are." But it's a well-known psychological phenomenon to unconsciously project the unacceptable parts of yourself onto someone else rather than taking responsibility for facing, owning and integrating those 'shadow' elements within yourself.

THE RELIEF OF BLAME

Lastly, probably the most irresistible payoff of all for holding on to your resentment is that it means you get to blame someone else for whatever is wrong, has been wrong and ever will be wrong in your life. Rather than taking 100% responsibility for the whole of your life, including your response to the past events that were beyond your control, you get to lay the blame at someone else's feet.

What I mean by taking responsibility for the past is that you need to find a way to come to terms with whatever has happened — however difficult or painful it might have been. I had many accidents when I was young. I broke my collar-bone, cut my leg open, knocked myself unconscious, lost my memory completely, dislocated and greenstick fractured several fingers etc. etc. Part of this was because I was a gymnast and some of it was adventurousness and not knowing or respecting my physical limits. Being repeatedly called 'Calamity Jane' by my parents may not have helped, but I didn't need to hold on to any resentment towards myself, or them, for what happened. That would literally have been adding insult to injury.

Ultimately, I am always responsible for myself even when I'm not consciously making decisions about how I react to something. I've given up blaming anyone else for how my life is and I've cut up my platinum 'get-out-of-anything-free' card of resentment.

WHEN SWEETNESS IS POISON

The taste of sugar releases morphine-like chemicals in the brain that are addictive. The brain also releases dopamine to imprint the memory of that to make sure we seek out the same experience again and again. The trouble is, we then get addicted to sugar.

I think resentment acts in the same way. What seems to be the sweetness of revenge, anger or resentment is ultimately a poison. Perhaps when enough research is done on the impact of the chemicals of emotion on our physiology we'll have evidence that resentment and holding on to negativity is as much of a threat to health as sugar.

The *most* important factor in all of this is to understand that all of the apparent benefits of holding on to resentment come at a very costly price. Most people are completely unaware there's any downside to holding onto resentment and not forgiving. This isn't surprising, given the miraculous multi-purpose uses of resentment.

RESENTMENT – LOVE KILLER

Resentment kills love slowly as it builds up over time. Resentment is the complete opposite of gratitude and appreciation. It's like focussing on everything you *don't* like about someone. Even when resentment is subtle or hard to notice, gradually it will stifle the flow of love between you and the other person until your focus is on everything that you think is 'wrong' about them, rather than what drew you together in the first place. This is most common in intimate partnerships, but it can happen between you and anyone you're in relationship with, including your kids. When resentment blocks the flow of love between you and those you care about, you all have a much less enjoyable experience of life.

Do you really want to have relationships that are running on:

- Avoidance and denial
- Self-protection (numbing out)
- Emotional distance
- Risk/Decision aversion
- Avoidance of compassion
- Self-pity
- Victimhood
- Martyrdom
- Self-righteousness
- Blame?

This *is* the experience most of us are having! And it's everywhere. Check out the news, the movies, the TV dramas, the arts, and so many songs. I'll bet you can hear the ego singing loud and clear.

Now you're aware of the games we all play with our egos, you can see how they need the fuel of resentment to thrive. You can also understand why forgiveness may be so low down on your to do list - if it is even on there at all. But once you understand all the multiple and significant downsides of carrying your resentment, forgiveness will seem more and more attractive!

Practice Suggestion: Start your list of everyone and everything you need to forgive. Include all those you love as well as those you despise or despair of. You could write down the number of years you've been holding resentment on each one and make a grand total of all your resentment years added together. This can be quite daunting and/or motivating! You could also make a note of any of the payoffs you think you might have been getting out of holding onto your resentment.

CHAPTER SEVEN
THE PRICE YOU'RE REALLY PAYING

"All blame is a waste of time.
No matter how much fault you find with another
and regardless of how much you blame him,
it will not change you."

Wayne Dyer

A TALE OF TWO SAUSAGES ...cont.

"Well," said the eldest daughter, taking a deep breath, *"Let me tell you all about it...."*

"When I was eleven, my dad..." she shot a disdainful glance in her motionless father's direction, *"...my dad stole two mini sausages off my plate before I had the chance to eat them without even asking me!"*

"I see," said the wise woman.

"I was saving them for last because they were my favourite," she explained.

"I see," said the wise woman again. *"And you've been carrying those particular sausages with you for all these years?"*

"Yes," she said, and proudly pointed out the hardest, blackest, smelliest sausages on the table. "I am hoping that eventually my father will understand what a terrible thing he did and properly apologise."

"I see," said the wise woman. "You're hoping that bringing your old sausages to the table year after year will make a significant contribution to his understanding?"

"Yyyeeessss," she said, sounding just a little uncertain by being questioned in this rational way.

"But that's not all he did," she went on, hoping to justify herself a little more. "He was mean. And he made me come home earlier than my friends when I went out. He wouldn't let me get my hair cut the way I wanted. And he criticised me all the time. And he wouldn't let me wear platform shoes and he never...."

As she spoke, she pointed to different parts of the pile of sausages and rotting things that she had built into the wall between her and her father. Her list of grievances continued on until she'd itemised pretty much every one of the things her father had ever done 'wrong'. All the mistakes he'd made, all the things she didn't like about him, everything about him that annoyed her, as well as all the things he hadn't done that she thought he should have done or could have done better. When she finished, she let out a long, deep breath and looked squarely at the guest. "You see?"

"Hmmmmmm, yes, I do see," said the wise woman, nodding at the eldest daughter to show she had listened and was considering her words carefully.

"Did you ever consider not bringing these grievances with you to Christmas dinner?" enquired the wise woman gently.

"Are you crazy!?" shrieked the eldest daughter. "No sausage wall!? How would I protect myself from his meanness?"

The wise woman rummaged underneath the detritus near her place setting and pulled out her shiny fork. She gently poked the wall and, instantly, the pile of mouldering food collapsed all over the table. "How is it helping you, exactly, dear?" she asked.

"Well…..," began the eldest sister, quickly beginning to re-build the sausages into a stronger wall shape, "…it just doesn't feel safe without it." TBC…

THE TRUE COST OF RESENTMENT – THE SIDE EFFECTS

From your ego's perspective, it might look like there are no advantages to letting go of your resentment. Why would you when there seem to be so many payoffs for holding on to it? But there are no *real* upsides to carrying resentment. All of the benefits that your ego thinks it's getting are imaginary. Every single one has devastating side effects. Ultimately, all of the apparent payoffs are really costs.

So perhaps, having read this far, you're now more aware of how your ego has been using the drug of resentment in your life and are starting to question what your resentment is costing you. Here are the most common ways your resentment can be ruining your life and slowly killing you in the process.

COST TO YOUR PHYSICAL AND EMOTIONAL HEALTH

This is the easiest place to notice where resentment is taking its toll on your life because you can feel it - in your body and your emotions.

As Bessel van der Kolk wrote in his introduction to *Trauma and Memory* by Peter Levine (2015), "For more than a century we have understood that the imprints of trauma are stored, not as narratives about bad things that happened in the past, but as physical sensations that are experienced as immediate life threats – right now."

It's widely known that stress kills. Carrying resentment is carrying stress 24/7, even if you're not consciously aware of it.

There may be other costs to your health, as in the case of my client whose son was disabled in an attack. Debra tried to stuff her feelings down with food and negatively impacted her health by overeating. Other ways to submerge your resentment might be beneath alcohol, drugs, spending too much time watching TV or surfing the internet, compulsive spending, gambling or being over-busy.

The impact of resentment on your emotional well-being might be the root cause of a persistent low-level feeling of unease that stops you feeling good about yourself and your life. Resentment can decrease your happiness levels so significantly that it can contribute to depression.

You might also be judging and condemning yourself for not being able to forgive. Then you'll be carrying guilt, shame and blame as well as the resentment. Letting go of all of that would be a significant emotional and physical relief...

COST TO THE QUALITY OF YOUR RELATIONSHIPS

You might experience the emotional cost of carrying your resentment in another subtle way. It might be limiting how deeply you let yourself feel or how open and engaged you are with the people in your life.

There's no doubt about it, resentment and lack of forgiveness can divide families, end friendships, spark generational feuds, cause divorce, split companies and provoke and sustain war.

You may know someone who has cut another person out of their lives completely, even if it's not directly happened to you. There are times (e.g. if there has been serious abuse) when this is the most healthy and sane response. But, you can choose to be out of contact with someone and still not harbour ill will against them. You can even wish them well. In many cases, though, a relationship is destroyed unnecessarily because people are unwilling to forgive.

The other way resentment might be affecting the quality of your relationships is if you are using resentment as a way to bond with others, by sharing and comparing stories and repeatedly ruminating on your misery and grievances. True intimacy and rich relationships are built on empathy, kindness, appreciation and the willingness to forgive.

RESENTMENT LEAKAGE

It's possible that your resentment might leak out into other relationships or affect unrelated areas of your life. I had a client who was feeling 'secondary' resentment towards their daughter when the person they were really angry with was their partner. This scenario is most likely to happen when you're angry with someone, but you don't resolve it with them directly. Then you find yourself taking out your grumpiness on something else; your dog, your child or another driver in a fit of road rage! Resentment can leak out as barbed humour, or in subtle acts of passive-aggression.

I had another client who was unknowingly being affected by this kind of resentment leakage. He had never forgiven his ex-wife for leaving him more than thirty years ago. Until we did the forgiveness process he had no idea that he had been resenting her so much. He also didn't realise there was a connection between his resentment, how he related to women in general and why he had never allowed himself to find a new relationship.

COST TO THE QUALITY OF YOUR PARTNERSHIPS

In Bruce Lipton's book, *The Honeymoon Effect*, he claims that it's possible to have a vibrant, healthy, perpetual 'honeymoon period' for the entire length of your most intimate relationship if you are able to stay consciously present with your partner.

The most destructive belief in any relationship is thinking that your happiness depends on the other person being a particular way. It plays out in every single relationship we have, but especially with our intimate partners. Every time someone doesn't meet our script for them, one more item gets added to the List of Grievances (L.O.G.). As the saying goes "Today's expectations are tomorrow's resentments."

If you can notice and let go of all the little grievances as they happen, you can keep your relationships resentment free. Even if a little resentment does build up over time, you can just take yourself through the forgiveness process and get free again.

Once you've done your Forgiveness Made Easy process, you might choose to have a clear 'non-violent communication' style conversation with the other person about the issue. I guarantee that if you have done your forgiveness work first, this will be much easier and more connecting. (See note and resources sections for further details.)

COST TO YOUR SEXUALITY AND YOUR EROTIC LIFE

If you have experienced any sexual abuse, it's very likely that your resentment (as well as the trauma itself) will have affected your sexuality ever since.

In cases of sexual trauma, I strongly recommend you get the qualified therapeutic help you need to process the experience before you engage with the forgiveness aspect of your healing. I also recommend you find someone who can work with you on the forgiveness process too. Please see the back of the book for more information on how to get help.

Even if you have never experienced any sexual abuse, carrying resentment towards another, especially if they are your sexual partner, will affect the quality and freedom of your sexual expression and enjoyment perhaps subtly, perhaps more obviously.

You may notice it in your lack of intimacy or desire, or in the absence of openness, joy, playfulness, surrender, enthusiasm, and depth of connection. Maybe you'll notice it in the tone of your voice, your lack of patience, or maybe you just don't feel as in love with your partner as you did before.

Sometimes problems in a relationship are simply the effects of the build-up of resentment rather than some fundamental incompatibility between two people. I wholeheartedly recommend trying a forgiveness process before you take any steps towards ending your relationship. However, if it is an abusive relationship you leave first, get to safety and then do your process work afterwards.

You might not be sexually active or in a sexual relationship right now. But human beings are able to have an erotic relationship with life itself. We have many senses, all of which are potential sources of pleasurable, joyful, playful, even ecstatic experiences.

If you're heaving a load of resentment around with you, your erotic response and engagement with life will be dulled and compromised. Whenever your heart and your body are closed down, you can't experience the finer, more sublime feelings like peace, joy, grace or especially gratitude.

COST TO YOUR FAMILY INHERITANCE

Because of our evolutionary nature - our capacity to keep growing and developing through the whole of our lives - it can feel as if we 'outgrow' our parents. We may question or reject their values and beliefs, and our adult relationship with them can be quite complex for many reasons.

In another of Bruce Lipton's books, *The Biology of Belief*, his research into epigenetics shows that the genetic codes in your cells can be changed by environmental factors. If you are not necessarily going to inherit the same diseases as your parents, you definitely don't have to live by their beliefs and prejudices - or take on second-hand resentment.

If habitual patterns of relating are still being played out, using resentment as the currency, nothing new can blossom in the relationship. You will be stuck behind your wall of resentment, unable to see beyond your limited perspective. You might maintain your resentful view of your parents for your whole life rather than go to the balcony to see and appreciate their good efforts. Holding onto your resentment will keep you acting out the same old behaviour patterns and this will prevent or limit any change in the way you relate to each other. This can destroy the entire relationship or, at best, reduce the quality and depth of connection within it. Forgiveness always works, whether your parents are still alive or not.

COST TO YOUR POWER

Letting go of your resentment might seem like you risk relinquishing some of your feeling of power. But it is false power. Your true power lies in being able to engage in life fully and spontaneously, completely free of your past.

When you hold onto your resentment, your behaviour is reactive and conditioned by your ego's demands and fears. You're not able to respond to the needs of the moment, to what is naturally arising, and explore new possibilities that lie on the other side of your shield of grievances.

Compare the level of tension in your body when you're lugging your suitcase through the airport, as opposed to when you're lying on a sun-lounger, holding onto nothing at all. Resentment is a burden and carrying it around 24/7 will *cost* you power - physically, emotionally and mentally. If you don't forgive and let it go, you will have taken your whole suitcase of resentment to the beach with you. Then, without even bothering to unpack in between, you'll take it on your visits to your relatives at Thanksgiving and / or Christmas. You're not fully available to the joys of the present moment because your energy is still entangled with your unresolved past.

As Gandhi said, "The weak can never forgive. Forgiveness is the attribute of the strong." It's practicing forgiveness that empowers you and *makes* you strong.

COST TO YOUR FREEDOM AND AUTONOMY

Carrying resentment comes at a cost to your personal freedom. I remember going to an all-day dance class and there was a guy there that I didn't want to connect with. For the whole day I made sure I always knew exactly where he was in the room relative to where I was. I was determined to avoid any possibility of being asked to partner with him for a dance. Everything I was doing was affected by my choice to always keep a certain distance away from him. I wasn't free to relax and enjoy the dance the whole day!

Resentment guarantees you're unconsciously acting out of old, unexamined behaviours. You may think you're being autonomous and independent, but you'll avoid a visit, cross the road, or sit at the opposite end of the table in order to minimise contact with a particular person.

Imagine a prison where you've safely incarcerated the person / people / thing you are resenting. Because you're the one who put them in there, you're also the one and only jailer. You have to stay in the prison 24/7 to make sure they don't escape. You're just as much a prisoner as they are. Just as trapped, just as limited.

COST TO YOUR PRODUCTIVITY AND CREATIVITY

Resentment will sap your energy and reduce your creativity and productivity. It can affect your freedom of expression, how deeply you connect with your feelings, your subject matter, your innovation and your execution. Every level of your creativity could be affected by the weight of your resentment.

Unresolved issues will play on your mind and make it difficult to concentrate or prioritise effectively. If you are resenting a colleague, it may be this, and not the other issues or excessive workload, that is weighing most heavily upon you. In the workplace, where egoic behaviour can be running the company, creating a culture where forgiveness is practiced can profoundly improve internal relationships and enhance productivity, as well as potentially create healthier triple bottom lines.

I'm also really curious about the direction the arts could take if our love affair with resentment was over. What other stories will we tell when we're able to create and collaborate beyond the limits of the ego and when we no longer run the world on the toxic superfuel of resentment, revenge, point-scoring, power games and one-upmanship?

COST TO YOUR SELF EXPRESSION

When you carry resentment, you might find yourself stuck behind your shield of grievance, avoiding challenging conversations which could disrupt the status quo. Your ego will not want you to risk hurting, upsetting, angering or losing people, so you might keep your conversations limited and inauthentic. You might withhold important feelings and thoughts or act in a passive-aggressive way and never actually say what's going on for you. Then you will feel an enormous build-up of tension because what you authentically feel and need to ask for never gets expressed and never gets heard. Any shut-down in your self-expression will impact the quality of your life.

I don't recommend expressing the *full* extent of years of resentment directly to the person concerned because they most probably won't be willing to sit there long enough to hear it. But when you use the Forgiveness Made Easy process in chapter nine, you will be able to fully express your feelings and consequently, become fully free.

Usually, your resentment will be based on your ego's unreasonable (or even reasonable!) expectations of the other person. Sometimes, however, you might need to clearly ask for what you need or give someone constructive feedback about their behaviour. I always recommend you do your forgiveness work first. Then you'll know what to say and will be able to communicate it clearly and cleanly without the charge of years of resentment built up behind it.

COST TO YOUR SELF-ESTEEM AND YOUR VALUES

Self-esteem is another concept like forgiveness that is easily misunderstood. You might feel as if you get esteem from carrying your resentment, because you're standing up for yourself and at least you're not like *them*. This is just more of the self-righteousness and specialness behaviour of the ego. The ego loves to be special or different from others for fear it won't be noticed or might be seen as insignificant.

Through my early training as a self-esteem mentor with the More to Life programme, I learned that the true meaning of self-esteem is unconditional positive regard for yourself just because you exist. You don't need to earn it - in fact you can't — being alive, being you is enough. True self-esteem doesn't go away even when you're feeling resentful, having a bad day or experiencing a challenging episode in your life. You can choose to love and accept yourself exactly as you are, simply *because* you are a human being. You can also treat yourself with unconditional positive regard, whether or not you have done anything in particular to 'deserve' it. Of course, it's OK to acknowledge yourself for your achievements in life and the qualities that you value in yourself. But you don't have to base your fundamental self-worth – and your self-identity - on what you have done, on your job title or qualifications or on being a fantastic lover / mother / boss / cook / athlete etc. Especially if your ego demands that you be multiple things at the same time. If you believe you are worthy of self-esteem only if and when you meet all the demands that you have of yourself (and / or that others have of you), then you will feel incredible pressure to be it all and have it all.

I don't even suggest that you base your self-esteem on the *qualities* you associate with being who you are. Not even the ones you like and value e.g. "I'm loving / noble / kind / intelligent" etc. This is because your ego can hijack these qualities and make them into something you identify with and might feel the need to defend. In essence, you're so much more than your qualities and personality quirks. If you can go to a party or meeting 'without your ego', you'll be free to not have to show up in any particular way. There will be no need to 'prove' yourself or be admired or liked, to look intelligent or kind, or be funny or creative. You can simply be fully present and available to enjoy every moment, knowing you're 'enough' just as you are.

The great thing about unconditional, true self-esteem is that the more you accept yourself exactly the way you are, as a growing, evolving being, the more you'll be able to treat others in the same way. Ultimately, everyone is worthy of unconditional positive regard even if you don't agree with their actions or condone their behaviour. This is fundamental respect for humanity and basic human rights. Then you can extend this unconditional positive regard beyond the human realm to all sentient beings and the planet we live on. This is what it could be like if we all lived without holding on to our resentment.

We judge ourselves in the process of judging others. Carrying resentment destroys our true self-esteem. It's hard to have unconditional positive regard for yourself when you are harbouring an arsenal of ill will against someone else and when you're playing ego games of who's right, who's wrong and who's the better person.

COST TO YOUR SPIRITUALITY AND PEACE OF MIND

If you have traditional spiritual beliefs, or think of yourself as a 'spiritual but not religious' person, resentment will cause you inner disquiet. All major spiritual traditions and secular ethics practices include compassion, love for others, understanding and forgiveness. If you have any kind of meditation or mindfulness practice, I guarantee that your resentment will be an obstacle to and disruptive factor in experiencing nirvana!

If you do have a particular faith, then carrying resentment will likely be costing you in the depth of your practice as a Buddhist / Sufi / Christian / Hindu / Yogi / Jew / Mystic etc.

I once worked with a member of the clergy who wept during his forgiveness process because he hadn't realised the depth and impact of his resentment, and what it had been costing him to carry it all through his life. Being a spiritual person doesn't mean forgiveness will naturally feel easy for you. It may even be harder for you to recognise and admit your resentment.

COST TO YOUR EVOLUTION

The stagnation of resentment pulls against the tides of your natural urge to evolve and grow as a human being. It will hamper your ability to progress in every area of your potential development. Holding on to resentment implies stuck thinking, stuck emotions, stuck perspective, no solutions, no movement and no growth.

You can't evolve beyond your ego without developing the capacity to forgive – to let go. Forgiveness is the most effective way to resolve inner and outer conflict. The act of refusing to hold ill will can be life-changing and can free you completely to move on from where you've been stuck in your life.

I often say to my clients that I can't *guarantee* any particular result, but I'm certain that if they don't do *anything* different, nothing will change inside of them and nothing will change in their outer circumstances either, other than by death or accident.

COST TO (YOUR) LIFE AFTER (THEIR) DEATH

Sometimes when I work with clients, they tell me it's too late to do anything about someone they're resenting because that person has already died. One of the wonderful things about the Forgiveness Made Easy process is that you can use it even after someone has died. You can resolve any 'unfinished' business even if someone died suddenly, or by suicide, or you never made peace between you when they were alive.

Sometimes we resent others for dying and the consequences of their death, but we rarely acknowledge or speak of it. Clients I've supported in these circumstances are often unaware of the guilt, anger and resentment that they're carrying along with their grief, and it's frequently turned against themselves.

Sometimes they wonder if they could have done something more or if they should have known or suspected something that would have made a difference to the outcome. They may be blaming themselves.

Sometimes, the work that needs to be done after someone has died, is us asking for forgiveness *from them* more than the other way around. Whichever way it is for you, carrying resentment against those who have died, or resentment against yourself, will always prevent you from reaching true resolution of the past and feeling peace in your heart.

COST TO YOUR PEACEFUL DEATH

Forgiveness powerfully offers the way for every single person to die a peaceful death. Of course, you can still die at any time, but if you've been doing your forgiveness work consistently, you'll have no unresolved emotional business and will already be at peace within yourself and in all your relationships. If you haven't done your forgiveness work, you may well feel regret instead of peace when you depart.

THE OTHER HAPPY ENDING

How ever you experience the emotional cost of carrying your resentment, whichever areas of your life it's impacting the most, you can get free of it entirely when you choose to forgive.

It really is possible – regardless of your circumstances. My amazing client Debra was able to completely forgive the youth who assaulted her son and left him permanently disabled. Afterwards, she wrote to me and said, *"Being able to let go of the past and move on seemed impossible to do before… [The forgiveness process] has allowed me to release and finally move on…. I think it will really help me for future emotional detoxing as I know how powerful the release can be."* The attacker was in prison and nothing changed about his conviction and nothing changed about the physical condition of her son, but something radical shifted in Debra's heart and body and her ability to engage with the ongoing challenges of her daily life.

I hope that now you are able to see the true price of carrying your resentment, you are longing to be able to let it go and truly set yourself free.

Practice Suggestion: Reflect on the areas of your life that might be affected by your resentments. Reflect on the impact of what it's costing you to hold on to your grievances. Imagine what it might be like to live your life free of all of this. Imagine in which areas of your life you might benefit the most.

* **Note**: I am indebted to K Bradford Brown and W Roy Whitten for their emphasis on the payoffs and costs of resentment, and want to acknowledge Anne Brown for permission to include those insights here.

PART THREE
HOW YOU CAN

"Forgiveness is not an occasional act; it is a permanent attitude."

Martin Luther King

CHAPTER EIGHT
PREPARING TO FORGIVE

"Forgiveness is not a feeling, but a decision to be free of ill-will. The feeling is relief."

K. Bradford Brown

A TALE OF TWO SAUSAGES...cont.

The wise woman made her Jedi gesture again and the eldest daughter fell into the waking trance. She turned towards the father, clicked her fingers in front of his face, and asked, "And how about you, Dear? You seem to have quite a fine collection of sausages of your own."

"Well, yes", he said, instantly awakening, "That's the thing! I did apologise to her, that very day, but I've never heard the last of it! And not only that, they were all very disobedient, cheeky children who didn't always do what they were told. My hair's turned grey, I've worried about them so much. They never thanked me properly either and they've cost me a lot of money over the years."

"I see," said the wise woman, looking at the middle-aged 'children' who were now sitting motionless at the table.

"And not only that..." The father proceeded to itemise the many failures of his children and all of his grievances against them. He then

went through everything he'd ever held against his darling wife and both dearly departed grandmothers. When he finished, the wise woman asked, "And how is your pile helping you exactly?"

"Well," said the father, "I think the children can jolly well tell I won't stand for their nonsense – I do have a pretty impressive pile."

"I see," said the wise woman. "You're hoping this might get them to respect you a little bit more? To help them understand the parental sacrifices you made over the years?"

"Yyyeeesssss...", replied the father, trailing off, sounding rather unconvinced about his own argument. TBC...

WHAT IT TAKES TO FORGIVE

We've been scrambling over the obstacles to forgiveness and, hopefully, you're convinced that there's no way to live with your resentment without suffering its toxic side-effects in every area of your life. Ill will will make you ill. No question.

Maybe you have a few last-minute reservations before you're ready to have a go at the forgiveness process itself. Even though you are on the brink of completely resolving the past and living your life free of relationship pain, your ego may still be cynically twisting its beard, unconvinced. That's OK.

In this chapter, I'll sum up all the important elements that need to be in place before you start your forgiveness practice. Then, in the next chapter, I'll outline the practice itself.

GOING OVER OLD GROUND

We started off with the obstacle of not having a useful definition of forgiveness itself, and the misunderstandings around what it is and is not. Then we explored the territory of vulnerability and all our fears around forgiveness. Then we took a look at the shenanigans of the ego - all of its delusions and habits, and the games that it likes to play. Then we revealed resentment for what it is - one of the most addictive and toxic feelings known to humankind.

Put all, or even some, of these obstacles together and it's no wonder that 85% of all those in the Gallup poll who said forgiveness was important also said they'd need help to do it. Given everything that can get in the way, it's a miracle anyone ever *does* forgive!

THE LAST FEW INGREDIENTS

There are several additional elements that can help make forgiveness even easier. They can make all the difference between authentic forgiveness – the kind that can change your life - and a half-hearted attempt like saying the words, "I forgive you", through gritted teeth. Forgiveness is only real when you *absolutely* refuse to hold any ill will against the other person. Imagine if you decided to drop your hands to your sides, with your palms open and facing outwards. No matter what I tried to give you to hold, everything would just fall to the floor. Letting go is like that. It's absolute. Or if you were helping me to climb up a mountain and I was dangling off the end of a rope with a long drop beneath me, I would have no doubt at all whether or not you had let go!

There's a quote in *A Course in Miracles* which says, "It does not matter 'how much' you have not forgiven them. You have forgiven them entirely or not at all." You've either let go or you haven't. Just like you can't be 'kind of' pregnant. You either are or you aren't. Be willing to let go of all of it!

OPEN MIND, OPEN HEART

The best approach to your forgiveness practice is with openness and curiosity. It really helps to have an open mind and an open heart. Be willing to question everything you've previously believed about forgiveness, as well as what you think might or might not be possible in relation to the person or thing you're forgiving. Your ego will probably object to the idea of forgiving. Go ahead anyway.

Keep an open mind about the process itself, too. It's a powerful visualisation and a significant event. You want to keep an open heart because, even though it's natural to pull away from pain, the only way for the pain to leave you forever is to face it and feel it as it releases through you.

You may well feel some emotions in the process of forgiving. That's OK. You'll be fine. This process will heal you. The steps of the process itself will hold you. You will feel much better afterwards. Hopefully you will feel 'smooth'.

In *The Untethered Soul*, Michael A Singer says, "When you feel pain, simply view it as energy... Do the opposite of contracting and closing. Relax and release... You will feel tremendous resistance to doing this... the heart will want to pull away, to close, to protect and to defend itself. Keep relaxing. Relax your shoulders and relax your heart. Let go and give room for the pain to pass through you. It's just energy. Just see it as energy and let it go."

DEEPENING YOUR INTENTION

The stronger and deeper your intention to forgive, the better. You might decide that you are doing this for your own sake – to finally get free of your past. You might do it for the sake of your health, your peace of mind, your creativity or just as an experiment. You can decide to forgive because you want to resolve the tension between you and someone else, or to change your family dynamic for the better. Or you can choose to forgive for the greatest good, because you want to stand up for peace and compassion in the world – starting with your own heart. You might want to set an example for your kids or colleagues, or you might want to use forgiveness as a spiritual practice. Whatever combination of reasons works to inspire you – choose those!

GRACE, GRIEF, GUIDANCE, GRATITUDE, GOODNESS, GOD (if you have one)

Finally, allow there to be all these 'Gs' in your process. Allow grace – forgiveness is an extraordinary process of undoing the past. Fully allow your grief – you may discover deep regret, sadness, pain or longing gets released as part of your process. Use whatever guidance you need – work with someone, use this book, get a forgiveness coach, invite your God (if you have one) and be prepared to experience the most extraordinary gratitude towards yourself once you've done your forgiveness work. You might even feel gratitude for the person you've been resenting, too. When you forgive, you may well feel plain old-fashioned goodness in your heart!

WHAT ELSE FORGIVENESS GIVES YOU

Besides the relief of living your life free of your past, the practice of forgiveness has the potential to develop many positive qualities in you. Forgiveness will develop your ability to take the leap from being one of the actors in the drama of your life, obediently playing out the script your ego has written, to seeing the whole play (including yourself) from the higher perspective of the balcony. From that wider, elevated view, you can see yourself and the events of your life much more objectively.

Through forgiveness, you practice staying open and curious, keeping what the Zen tradition calls a 'beginners mind'.

Forgiveness will teach you how to put yourself in another person's shoes. This has the potential to transform the quality of every relationship you have. According to American philosopher and writer Ken Wilber, taking the perspective of other is a foundational skill necessary for us to evolve as human beings and become 'superhuman'.

The capacity to set yourself free from your own perspective, and question your interpretation of events, allows you to develop deeper compassion and empathy, and even feel loving kindness toward the other person and their experience. I can't remember a single client whose abuser hadn't also been a victim of significant trauma or some kind of abuse themselves. Forgiveness breaks the chain.

Knowing that you can choose to act for the greater good will strengthen your faith in your highest human potential. I have felt humbled many times as I witness my clients forgive all kinds of challenging circumstances from betrayal and abuse to neglect. Forgiveness is a testament to the true nobility of the human heart. Forgiveness will also increase your ability to trust in yourself, others and life.

You trust yourself more, because you recognise you have the power over whether or not you hold ill will against someone. You take 100% responsibility for your life now.

You can also trust others more whenever you are able to communicate with the very highest in them. When you do this in the Forgiveness Made Easy process, you invite others to express from their highest, most compassionate selves which naturally includes their shame, remorse and apology.

And as you forgive and let go of the past, you loosen your grip on demanding life be a certain way in order for you to be happy. You learn to be more flexible and adaptable to the true needs of the moment (including yours) and experience the freedom of holding on to nothing from the past.

Forgiveness will develop your inner strength. As you choose the *non-doing* of letting go you will become increasingly free of your own ego as well as from the effects of everyone else's ego. That's a very powerful way to live your life.

Forgiveness will develop your courage as you learn to face what needs to be faced. It also develops self-awareness and a radical honesty about the subtle (and usually unconscious) games you've been playing. You learn all about the wheeling and dealing of the ego (yours and everyone else's) and the ways it tries to protect your self-image. Then you can courageously take full responsibility for your choices.

You'll also be exercising your willingness to be honest with yourself about your ego, your feelings, your judgements, your assumptions, and your not-always-loving responses. Forgiveness encourages development of the strength and humility to face up to your actions. With humility, comes empathy and you might even be able to see that in certain circumstances, it's possible you could have done a similar thing.

When you face your past, or a challenging present, you will feel empowered just by the act of facing it. In the process of forgiveness, you will see that it is you who is giving these circumstances and people all the meaning they have for you. This gives you the ability to take that wider perspective and get to the heart of what's really going on. You develop the ability to be discerning and more objective about other people's behaviour. When you have clarity about the situations in your life, you'll be less reactive because you won't take them so personally. As you witness how your resentment is adversely affecting your life, you will see you always have the power to choose whether or not to forgive.

KEEPING A LIST

Your first step is to choose someone from your list that you want to forgive. The reason I recommend keeping a list is because forgiveness work hardly ever seems like an urgent priority. If you notice you're feeling resentful and want to deal with it, but don't have time straight away, just jot it down on your list and then make the time to do your work when you can.

This develops a couple of important capacities. First, you will be noticing your ego at work. You'll learn to feel the subtle movements of your heart as it opens to the things you love, appreciate and desire, and closes to the things you judge, abhor and deny. Second, your list reminds you that your heart matters to the whole. When you choose to practice forgiveness in your life, you benefit not just those closest to you, but through the interconnectedness of everything, you serve the whole world.

In Stephen Covey's *7 Habits of Highly Effective People*, he describes four quadrants – things to do are divided into QI: urgent & important, QII: not urgent but important, QIII: not important but urgent and QIV: not important and not urgent.

Forgiveness processing is most likely to fall into quadrant II – not urgent, but important – because it has transformational potential. Work through your list and take the time to forgive each one. You may have to challenge the habits of a lifetime to add, "Forgiveness process on ...." to your to-do list e.g. forgiving the person who smashed your car window and stole your purse. But it will be worth your time and effort.

I have often done my forgiveness work when I'm alone, walking in a secluded place, or on a long car journey, where I can speak freely, out loud. Sometimes I'll work on something that's come up recently. If I haven't cleared down my list, I'll work on that, or sometimes I'll just do a little housekeeping on the person I'm going to meet, work with or visit next.

It's not that I'm a phenomenally resentful person (so far as my ego tells me!) – just that I do have an ego. I make judgements and assumptions and sometimes wish other people or circumstances were different from how they are. When I use the superpower of forgiveness, I free myself. I make amends if necessary. I take responsibility for any meaning I've given to the situation that's not true, like "They don't care about me" or "I don't matter", and remind myself of what *is* true and take a stand to live by that. I return to a sense of peace and harmony within myself and release all that energy for my creative projects (rather than plotting revenge...). Once you're familiar with the steps of the Forgiveness Made Easy process, you'll be able to do your forgiveness work anytime and anywhere that works for you.

LETTING GO OF THE PAST

Letting go of the past is not only the *outcome* of your forgiveness work, but also part of how you get there. When you choose to think of your past differently, you also choose to let go of hoping to get anything from the other person. They may never know the full extent of how their behaviour affected you. They may never apologise or take responsibility or make amends for what they did or didn't do. You stop waiting for them to change or do something different and just go ahead and forgive them anyway.

If you let go of your end of the rope in a game of tug of war the game is over. The tension is resolved. If you no longer carry your grievances about the past, you don't have to try to forget what happened. You're at peace with it. You can honour the past by accepting what happened, accepting your feelings and reactions and not be in denial about any of it.

I had a client who felt she couldn't forgive because she was afraid she would be dishonouring her ancestors. All of her relatives, except one grandmother, died in the gas chambers of Auschwitz. As we worked through her process, she realised that the hate in her heart for the Nazis was the same hate that had driven the atrocities in Auschwitz. By holding onto her resentment, she was perpetuating the war, even though it had been over for decades. All that anger and hatred was subtly still alive in her, two generations on.

The past doesn't have to define your future. You never have to experience what you went through, ever again. You can't have an exact repeat experience of your childhood traumas, anyway. Even if behaviour patterns that were put in place during your childhood are still evident in your behaviour as an adult, you have choices today that you didn't have as a child. Your genes, your memories and your behaviour are all open to change. Forgiveness is the secret release mechanism that will free and resolve the trapped pain of the past forever.

QUESTION YOUR BELIEFS

Our brains are programmed to find patterns and relationships between things. It's why you can see faces in random patterns on your curtains. Unfortunately, we are also very prone to misleading ourselves.

One client I worked with had lost a parent at a very young age. He remembered being asked to fetch some medicine, and because the medicine hadn't worked, he believed that his father's death was his fault. He also seemed to have made other meanings at this point like, "I can't be relied upon", "I'm bad", or "I'm powerless". None of these core beliefs were true, but they were unconsciously still having an effect on his adult behaviour. He wept for a long time with relief and was able to forgive himself, when he realised, as part of his process, that his father's death had not been his fault.

Through engaging with the process of forgiveness, you may be able to uncover some of your own deeply-buried limiting beliefs, and free yourself from them.

ALL YOU NEED TO FORGIVE

Here's a quick re-cap of the important things you need to remember about forgiveness:

- ✓ Forgiveness is for *you* first and foremost.
- ✓ Forgiveness is: *"The absolute refusal to hold ill will against someone (or something) for what they did or didn't do."*
- ✓ Forgiveness isn't condoning anything, or in place of restorative justice.
- ✓ Expect and allow resistance from your ego. Go ahead anyway.
- ✓ Follow the steps of the process, with support if you need it.
- ✓ Be prepared to feel a little vulnerable as you do your process.

One of my spiritual teachers, Craig Hamilton, created a list of Principles of Evolutionary Culture, one of which is particularly useful and applicable for approaching your forgiveness practice; "If you're not uncomfortable, you're probably not evolving." This speaks of the egoic discomfort you experience every time you stretch beyond one of your comfort zones or challenge your ego's beliefs and limitations. This feeling of living on the edge of what might be possible, beyond the confines of your ego, can feel a little scary. Resistance and a little discomfort are understandable and to be expected. The really important thing to remember is that feeling your feelings won't kill you whereas NOT feeling them, and never resolving your emotional issues, eventually might...

If you have suffered trauma and/or abuse and feel that you need support to forgive a significant event or person, please do get help. For more information about how to find a forgiveness coach, please see the back of the book.

READY TO FORGIVE

Hopefully you're now feeling better equipped and ready to do a forgiveness process. You have a definition of forgiveness that works, you understand your ego's fears and concerns about being vulnerable and you appreciate how toxic and addictive the poison of resentment truly is. You know who and what you need to forgive and your deepest intentions for why you need to forgive them – so you can finally get free from your past. Now you just need to decide on the where, the when and the how.

There really aren't any downsides to forgiving and letting go of your past. So, if you're about as ready as you'll ever be to do your process, I am delighted to offer you my Forgiveness Made Easy method. I trust it will serve you well.

Practice Suggestion: Reflect on what you might gain from doing a forgiveness process. What could change for you? Consider and write down what your deepest intentions are for doing your work. Ask yourself, "Why do I want to forgive this person?" and write down your answer. Then repeat this enquiry several times, dropping down deeper and deeper each time. "I choose to forgive ………… because ………." and "I choose this because……." Keep going until you've gone as deep as you can go and you're anchored in your deepest motivations for going ahead. Then do whatever else you need to do to prepare yourself for the process in the next chapter.

CHAPTER NINE
THE FORGIVENESS MADE EASY PROCESS

*"When we are no longer able to change a situation,
we are challenged to change ourselves."*

Viktor E. Frankl

WHERE AND WHEN

It's up to you when you do your forgiveness process but the sooner the better! You need to feel somewhat ready, even if you still have reservations and your inner voice is piping up with unhelpful thoughts like, "They don't deserve my forgiveness", or "This will never work." The best thing to do is just try the process and see what happens. All you have to lose is your resentment!

It's important to choose the right time and place to do your Forgiveness Made Easy process. You need to choose a time when you have long enough to complete the practice and a place that feels private and safe.

As I've mentioned before, if you have experienced significant emotional or physical abuse, please do not do this process alone – get support.

Some people find they go deeper and have a more profound experience when they're being supported. It could be a trusted friend or advisor, a spiritual guide, a forgiveness coach, or a Journey therapist. They may have a perspective you don't and can help you to see some of the ego games that are at play, which are often hard to spot by yourself. Also, there is something wonderfully reassuring about having someone else witness your process and not take it personally, reject you or run away screaming because of it.

If someone else is listening with compassion and understanding, then their presence will be a real support to your process. You might like to set up a 'forgiveness swap' with a friend, and take it in turns to do your process and support each other through it. I've been doing this for years and my 'process support' friends still speak to me and bring me gifts on my birthday, even though they know the depths to which my ego will stoop when I'm at my most resentful!

Most importantly, _don't_ try doing this process face to face in real life with the person you are resenting. If they have an ego (which they will unless they are enlightened) this will get in the way of your process. If there's something that needs to be communicated, sorted out, or litigated for, then you can do that *after* your process, once you are free of your resentment.

There's a very interesting book by Brad Blanton, *Radical Honesty*, that recommends a face-to-face practice of complete honesty. For now, I would err towards just taking care of your resentment work by yourself or with your forgiveness coach / mentor / friend. Otherwise, if you are confident and happy to go ahead by yourself, it is completely OK for you to work alone. Many people do and they have great success.

ENOUGH TIME

Once you get going on saying everything that needs to be said as part of your forgiveness process it can often expand and turn out to be more than you imagined. The length of the process will depend to a certain extent on how long you've been carrying the resentment for, and how much detail you go into, as well as how fast you speak. Generally, the longer and more closely you've known the person, or endured a situation, the more time it will take.

If you rush through any part of the process, you won't feel as if you've really resolved the issue. It really is worth taking plenty of time, particularly over the most significant resentments you carry, so that you can fully experience freedom and release when you've finished.

This probably goes without saying, but also turn off all your electronic devices. Give your 100% wholehearted attention to the process and don't try to multi-task.

THE IMAGINARY CONVERSATION

The forgiveness made easy process is set up as an imaginary conversation with the person you want to forgive. Suggesting an imaginary conversation may sound simplistic, but just as the placebo effect works *even if you know you are taking a placebo*, so this process works too. Even though you know you're imagining what's happening and making it all up, it will still work.

The brain can't actually tell the difference between what you perceive 'out there' in the world and what's going on in your imagination. If you watch someone dancing, your brain fires up the same as if *you* were dancing. Studies in brain science have shown that the effects of *imagining* yourself exercising can actually increase muscle size by about 1/3 even if you're not doing any exercise at all.

When you watch a movie, you know you're sitting in your seat looking up at a screen because you bought your ticket on the way in. You know the characters aren't real and the story isn't true, yet you care enough about what happens that you'll laugh, or cry, or feel afraid even though none of it is really happening. Your experience of your feelings is *always* real, even if the events that are evoking them are not.

An imaginary conversation makes the process completely safe because you don't have to confront the abusive person in real life. You can say things freely in the imaginary realm. You can speak authentically from your heart and from the pain of whatever has remained unspoken and unresolved. In an imaginary conversation, you can resolve past issues with people who have died, or committed suicide or who are untraceable. Nothing is unresolvable in the realm of your imagination.

You might want to think of this conversation as a ceremony or ritual and take a few moments to honour what you are about to do. You are about to forgive, which is a master spiritual and emotional intelligence practice. Forgiveness is a deep expression of courage, honesty, vulnerability, humility, compassion, emotional strength, empathy and unconditional love. As my friend Ralph once said, "Forgiveness is pretty much a one-word distillation of all spiritual, philosophical and emotional practice." Ultimately, it's an act of empathy and understanding. Even if you still don't think the person you need to forgive deserves your forgiveness, *you* deserve to set yourself free by forgiving them.

You may have more than one person or past experience you'd like to forgive, but for now, just choose the one that is most important to you. Even though it is possible to forgive several people at once, I suggest doing just one at a time.

You might like to read through the whole process before you start. Alternatively, you can listen to a free mp3 of me guiding you step-by-step through the process, which you can also download from: *www.forgivenessmadeeasy.co.uk/bookbonus*. These are the steps:

1. **Start Where You Are** - Visualise Eye to Eye
2. **Talk** – Heart to Heart
3. **Switch Positions** – Shoe to Shoe
4. **Go Higher** – Observe and Express from the Balcony
5. **Expose Your Ego's Payoffs and Costs** – The Haggling
6. **Forgive and Let Go** – The Antidote and Resolution
7. **Complete** – Next Steps

STEP 1. START WHERE YOU ARE - VISUALISE EYE TO EYE

Sitting in a comfortable, relaxed position, allow your eyes to gently close. If you feel uncomfortable or unsafe closing your eyes, then you can do the whole process with your eyes open. Just drop your eyes and soften your gaze so that you are in a semi-meditative state.

Take the time to become fully present, awake and aware of wherever and however you are right now. Take a few deep breaths and notice all of the physical feelings and sensations in your body. Take a scan of your physical state from the inside. Notice if there are any places of tension in your body, any feelings of pain or contraction or particular areas of your body that draw your attention. Allow yourself to notice those places where you feel physical sensations, like pain or tingling and those parts of your body where there's numbness or not much feeling at all.

Then gently bring your awareness to your emotional state. Notice the subtle movement of inner feelings or waves of emotion, however slight they might be. Notice where you have emotional feelings in your body, including numbness or *lack* of feeling, as well. Fully allow whatever emotional experience is here in this present moment. You may feel more than one emotion, or conflicting emotions. Using your breath, just relax and soften and allow everything to be exactly the way it is.

Then bring your awareness to your mind and all of your mental activity. Let go of any preconceptions about how the process should be and any judgements or expectations. Don't focus on any thought or idea in particular, just keep allowing everything to be exactly the way it is. Keep a 'beginner's mind'. Forget everything you think you know about forgiveness and be open and curious about what might arise – which might not be what you expect. Allow yourself to be aware of your mental activity, but don't get involved in any of it. Just stay present, open and aware.

Even though you're dealing with events and resentment from the past, you are actually bringing everything to the present moment – the only place where anything can ever be fully resolved. This moment is the liquid edge of life - the furthest edge of time that evolution has reached. This is where the meanings you are making can be questioned, the past can be undone and a new future can emerge.

You need to give this process your full attention so that you can receive the greatest benefit from it. The more still and silent you are within yourself before you begin, the deeper and more profound your process will be.

Finally, staying aware of your breath, bring to mind the person or thing you are about to forgive and feel into your body's response. Put your attention on the part of your body where you feel yourself holding your resentment and breathe into it. If your mind shows you an image that represents the resentment (like a wall or a shield) just notice that too.

STEP 2. TALK – HEART TO HEART

Sit quietly, relaxed, softening, allowing and accepting all of your experience exactly the way it is in this moment. Begin to visualise a safe space *inside* yourself where you will conduct your process of forgiveness.

The most obvious place to imagine doing this work is in your heart or the place in your body where you're feeling or seeing the resentment. If your imagination shows you a different safe space altogether, go with that. It may be a beautiful garden, a clearing in some woods, a deserted beach or a peaceful, safe room inside a building.

You can't get this wrong. Just go ahead and allow your imagination to show you the best place for you to do the process. It may be different each time you do it. Trust yourself. As a rule of thumb, don't second guess yourself either. The psyche is phenomenally powerful and your imagination will reveal its own path to healing if you trust it. Let your imagination show you what's going to work best for *you*.

Next, imagine sitting beside a fire. I like the metaphor of having the warmth and protection of a fire because then anything that needs to be resolved or discarded can be thrown into it and transmuted.

When I first began doing my forgiveness work, I imagined a special 'forgiveness' chair that was an old-fashioned green velvet, wing-backed chair beside a roaring log fire. Just allow your imagination to offer you whatever feels most appropriate for your process.

Once you feel you're sitting comfortably, with some kind of sacred flame – a fire or a candle – to represent the presence of light, invite the person you need to forgive to come into the scene and sit down with you. Then, in your imagination, make eye contact with them and sit for a few moments together in silence.

When you're ready, begin to speak out loud, heart to heart, saying everything that needs to be said. This is the most important part of the process. Give yourself complete permission to say whatever needs to be said, especially those things that were never spoken at the time. You might use any or all of these sentence stems:

- "I feel angry with you because…"
- "I resent you for all the times when…"
- "I hate you for…"
- "I wish…"
- "Why…?"
- "Thank you for…" because sometimes there's a need to thank someone first before you feel you can speak about your resentment. This is especially true when the relationship is complex, or if the other person helped, as well as challenged or hurt, you.

This process is most effective when it's done out loud. Even though you could do this practice as a written exercise, there is a unique release that comes from fully expressing yourself vocally. Not just 'as if' you've said something, but allowing yourself to actually *say* what needs to be said out loud. There is real power in hearing yourself say what is true from your perspective, too. There is also power in imagining that it's being heard – possibly for the first time.

Say anything and everything, everything, everything that has, up until now, been unexpressed. Give yourself permission to be completely uninhibited about what you say - even things that you would never dream of saying to the person face-to-face. Say all those things you wish you'd said at the time and things you didn't even know how to say back then. Say out loud the most honest, authentic, exposing admission of whatever you've been holding in your heart, in your throat and in your body. You might include things you've already said before, but didn't think the other person fully heard.

Allow yourself to be petty, not make sense, swear, and be politically or spiritually incorrect. Just be real and keep going until you feel you have expressed everything. If in doubt, admit it and allow it. Including "I can never forgive you for that", if that is how you feel at this point in the process.

Give yourself permission to feel all of your feelings, even if they don't make sense, aren't congruent, conflict with each other and/or are deeply uncomfortable. You might be moved to tears if you're doing this work authentically. Don't be afraid to feel your feelings, let them move through you and experience them fully so that they can be resolved.

If you would normally speak in a different language (like your native tongue) to the person you are addressing this can be even more powerful than translating your words into a second language. Go ahead and choose whichever language feels most authentic and expressive for you.

This is the longest part of the process and the most important. If you don't include everything - the minor irritations as well as the bigger grievances and injuries - you will find it harder to let it all go. In my first process on my mother, one of the petty things I confessed that I resented her for was wearing pop-socks! But the heart of my resentment was about her illness and its devastating effect on her health, our relationship and our whole family.

In order to let go of all your resentment, you first need to acknowledge you've been holding on to it. Every little piece matters. When you get to see the full extent of the resentment you've been carrying, it will help to convince you to let it all go.

Include all the ways you might have treated the other person badly or used your resentment against them to justify your behaviour, e.g. "I used my resentment against you to justify stealing stationery from the office".

You might not remember some important things until after all of the little things have been said. I worked with one woman who at the very end added, "Oh, and I resent you for saying you wanted to kill yourself when I was nine years old." It was almost an after-thought, but it turned out to be the most impactful part of her childhood trauma and, understandably, one of the major reasons for her resentment.

If in doubt, give yourself a little extra time. Keep making eye contact with the person you are working on and check in with your body until you are sure you feel completely 'empty' of all your resentment and have said everything else you want to say.

STEP 3. SWITCH POSITIONS – SHOE TO SHOE

Once you've said everything you need to say, the next step is to acknowledge that the other person may have something they wish to say in response to your communication. Take your time and switch positions. Put yourself in their shoes and allow yourself to reply out loud from their perspective. Ask yourself what they might say and then speak those words out loud. Their authentic response might be defensive, or dismissive, or they might be silent and unresponsive. They might make excuses about their behaviour or they might apologise. They might not do anything at all and that's also OK.

Then switch positions again and respond to what they just said. Keep going if more resentment comes up (check your back pockets!) until you've said everything you need to in reply. Keep going until everything that needs to be said between you has been communicated and heard.

STEP 4. GO HIGHER
– OBSERVE AND EXPRESS FROM THE BALCONY

This time both of you slip out of the shoes of your egos and 'go to the balcony' to take a wider perspective.

Reach inside for the highest, wisest part of yourself. This is the part of you that's aware of your inner dialogue, the meaning you're making, and all of your feelings. It never gets involved with the dramas of your life, but witnesses the whole experience.

Now ask the other person to reply to everything you have said from *their* highest, wisest self, from their deepest heart and soul. This is the self they would be if they had been given perhaps a different up-bringing, different opportunities and loving, wise guidance.

Even if you don't believe that person has a higher, wiser self, keep going higher and, if necessary, reach so high you go beyond the personality of the person altogether. If this is something you just can't get past on your own, then I recommend that you work with a forgiveness coach, or a Journey therapist, or someone who can support you through your process.

Ideally, from this higher perspective, the other person will be able to see the consequences and impact of their behaviour. They will experience enough compassion and remorse to spontaneously say that they are sorry for what they've done. They might even break down in tears as they acknowledge their behaviour and the harm it has caused.

Strangely, even though this is just an imagined process, this part can seem so authentic and real that the apology can feel as powerful as if it happened in real life. Being able to witness the other person's remorse is deeply healing. Ask yourself, "What did I most want to hear them say at the time, or would love to hear them say now?" Let them say that from their highest self too.

Then say what else needs to be said from your highest self, in response to that. Let the other person respond from their highest self and allow the conversation to move naturally between you. Sometimes, profound and surprising insights can be experienced at this stage in the process.

Continue until it feels as if everything has been fully expressed and you're ready to move to the next step, which is to honestly and humbly examine the payoffs and costs of your resentment.

STEP 5. EXPOSE YOUR EGO'S PAYOFFS AND COSTS – THE HAGGLING

Even if you feel ready to forgive without doing this key part of the process – still take the time to do it.

Exposing your ego's payoffs and costs is one of the most powerful parts of the process and can make letting go of your resentment much easier. It will remind you why your ego has been hanging on to the resentment and the price you've been paying for it. It takes deep humility and self-honesty to own up to all the apparent benefits you might have been getting from your resentment. This is another part of the process where you may feel temporarily quite uncomfortable. Go ahead anyway.

Think about all the different aspects of your life and from your highest, wisest self, say out loud to the other person every single way in which holding on to your resentment has been serving your ego. It could be a sense of superiority, justification for doing whatever the hell you like, a victim or martyr story, avoiding making an important decision, the illusion of self-protection and so on. See chapter six for a recap on this. If you can be honest and admit all the secret games your ego has been playing you will see the payoffs for what they really are – just costs in disguise.

Then, from your highest perspective, truthfully say out loud all the ways holding on to your resentment is costing you more than you're willing to pay. Refer to chapter five and chapter seven for a reminder of the subtleties of this. If you're doing this correctly, you will *want* to forgive - maybe even urgently - because once you realise that all your apparent payoffs are actually costs there is *no benefit* to carrying resentment and not forgiving. *No benefit at all – only costs.* Any protection you might seem to be getting from holding on to your resentment will be *costing* you in your intimacy and depth of connection with others etc. Your resentment will be impacting every area of your life. When you feel complete with this part, you may like to invite the other person's highest, wisest, self, to respond in some way.

STEP 6. FORGIVE AND LET GO
– THE ANTIDOTE AND RESOLUTION

Next, maintain eye contact with the person you're forgiving in your imaginary scene and say out loud the most meaningful words you can find to express your forgiveness of them. Remember that forgiving them means only that you are refusing to hold any ill will against them for what they did or didn't do. You are forgiving the *person*. You're not saying you condone their behaviour or that they were right and you were wrong, or that you want to reconcile with them. You are choosing to *let go of your ill will*. You can still keep clear, strong, loving boundaries and take a stand against any injustice that may have been done.

You can be specific and say, "I forgive you for not being there when I needed you...", or it can be more general, e.g. "I wholeheartedly forgive you completely and utterly for everything." If it helps, you can include a phrase like, "Even though I don't agree with what you did, and even though I may not ever understand it, I refuse to carry any ill will against you for a moment longer. I completely and utterly free myself of my resentment. I free you and forgive you absolutely, body, heart and soul."

If you don't feel ready to do this, or feel resistance or are unable to truly forgive, it may be that you have more unexpressed resentment. I recommend returning to the FIRST step again and express any additional resentment, any new associated payoffs, and costs, and then try again.

After you have offered your forgiveness, if it feels appropriate, you can also ask the other person to forgive you for anything that you might need to be forgiven for. This could include how you've resented them, or held them in contempt, or treated them with disdain. If this is the case, don't forget to forgive yourself too.

When I did a series of processes on my past relationships, the emphasis of the majority of the conversations was my asking for forgiveness from *them* for all the ways in which I'd been difficult, unconscious, unloving and unkind. I also asked for forgiveness for all of the ways I'd judged and treated them because of the resentment I carried.

If in doubt, include it all in your conversations. Stay authentic and humble and keep going until you feel a sense of release and relief.

STEP 7. COMPLETION – NEXT STEPS

When you're complete with that part of the visualisation, allow yourself to experience what it's like to be free from carrying all that resentment. Feel into the sweet release of forgiveness. Hopefully, you will be feeling much lighter.

If it's helpful, imagine yourself stepping up to the fire holding your ill will in your hands. Your imagination could depict it in any way, e.g. that huge sofa-cushion, a dark shield of grievance, the wall of sausages, stones in your shoes, a big boulder, the squashed teddy you've been carrying or a knife taken out of your wound. See yourself throwing whatever it is into the fire to be burned up and transmuted.

You can also throw in all the pain and beliefs and unhealthy behaviour patterns that came out of your experience with that person. Put into the fire everything you need to let go of and watch it all burn away to nothing.

Looking at the other person now, free from your resentment, you may wish to make a pledge for how you intend to treat them from now on. You could make a new commitment about how you want to behave in that relationship (especially if it's ongoing) or how you want to be as you remember that person. "From this moment on, how I choose to treat you/think of you is…" Whenever you look at them or think of them in the future, you can have an intention to look 'through' their personality self and connect with them higher self to higher self.

If it feels appropriate, you may wish to tell the other person what you appreciate about them and what you're grateful for. There may be some circumstances where this will not be relevant or feel natural, even after you've forgiven them. Trust your sense of what feels in alignment with your highest values. Check in with your body to make sure you are feeling 'smooth' and that there's nothing else left unsaid, unconfessed, or unresolved.

Then in your imagination, surround that person with golden light and allow their image to dissolve and disappear into it. You may then wish to sit for a moment alone by the fire in your imagination and see if your higher, wiser self has anything it wants to give you or say to you.

Check to see how your heart looks and feels now (or whichever imaginary place you saw when you originally spoke to the other person). Feel into the part of your body where you were holding your resentment when you started the process and sense what's loosened up, changed or resolved.

Then imagine yourself going forward with this forgiveness in your heart, completely free of all your resentment. See yourself in your life in the days and weeks ahead and feel into what has changed. What's new for you? What's become possible? How are you feeling about your past now? If this is an ongoing relationship, how are you seeing yourself being different within it? How do you feel towards this person and about your life without your resentment?

Give yourself a little time at the end of your process to come back to the present moment. Put your hand on your own heart, feel the warmth under your hand and allow yourself to gently return to awakened, grounded awareness. Take a couple of deep breaths. Feel your feet on the floor, feel your spine and feel your hands. Feel the forgiveness inside you, fully integrated, and your heart, light. You may want to make a few notes in a journal, especially if you had a clear vision of how things might be different for you in the future. Or just take time to be quiet and reflect on the amazing process you've just done.

AFTER FORGIVENESS

This may seem like a very long process, but actually, it doesn't have to take all that long. The most important thing to remember is that it will be worth your time and energy to become truly free. Nothing else can bring the same benefits as forgiveness.

Often clients will tell me that even though they've done a lot of work on themselves, and on that relationship or issue, they've never really felt like they've forgiven the person completely before, even after many years of therapy.

You may still need to have a real-life face-to-face conversation with that person *after* your forgiveness process, if you have something important to communicate. I suggest that you are sensitive to the time and place you choose for that conversation as well as what you say and how you say it.

If you have serious concerns about meeting face to face, you could ask to have a mediated meeting with a trained facilitator, or a specialist in relationship counselling. Otherwise, it might be enough to study something like Marshall Rosenberg's nonviolent communication techniques (NVC) before having your conversation.

If the person you've forgiven continues to treat you in an unhealthy or unacceptable way, you may need to make a different choice about whether you stay in relationship with that person (if you have that option) or how much contact you want to have with them going forward.

CONSTANT RESOLUTION

You may need to do more than one process on someone. My mother died over 23 years ago, and recently I did a deep and profound forgiveness ceremony with her after another layer of my resentment came up, which was to do with how I was treated as a baby.

Don't be deterred – it's always worth repeating the process. One time, I'd just done some forgiveness work on a friend of a friend whom I didn't really like that much even though a couple of people said they thought we'd get on. Later that day, I walked into a local shop and she was standing at the counter. She made a remark that implied that I had pushed in front of her and I got completely re-triggered by her again!

So, I added her back onto my list, did my forgiveness work once more, and a relatively short time after that, she and I began working together. Since then, we've become very close friends and we regularly support each other with our forgiveness work.

WHAT'S NEXT

Once you've worked through everyone on your list, keep practicing! Every time you notice you need to do some forgiveness work, just do it and your heart will become a war-free zone – a garden of peace. Forgiveness work is the best practice for keeping all your ongoing relationships healthy. Your personal forgiveness work will ultimately serve everyone by breaking the habitual patterns of resentment that have plagued humanity for centuries. You will be making a significant contribution to the global evolution of human consciousness. I'll say more about this in the final chapter.

I honour you for being willing to radically change your life, and change the world for the better, with your practice of forgiveness.

Practice Suggestion: Pick someone or something and do your process! Book a session with a friend or with a forgiveness coach. Download or listen along to the FREE mp3 of the Forgiveness Made Easy process and let me guide you step-by-step through the process:

www.forgivenessmadeeasy.co.uk/bookbonus

CHAPTER TEN
TROUBLESHOOTING

"Between stimulus and response, there is a space.
In that space is our power to choose our response.
In our response lies our growth and our freedom."

Viktor Frankl, *Man's Search for Meaning*
(original title in German:
Saying Yes to Life in Spite of Everything)

A TALE OF TWO SAUSAGES ...cont.

With a wave of her hand and a click of her fingers the wise woman asked, "And how about you, dear?" extending her kind enquiry to each family member in turn.

She listened to each one of them explain why they had gathered their particular collection of decomposing artefacts for the Christmas table and why they thought it would help make their family relationships better.

When everyone had finished, the wise woman clapped her hands. The soul of the father and eldest daughter changed places. From his daughter's point of view, the father could see that he had made a few mistakes and hadn't understood his daughter very well. From her father's point of view, the eldest daughter could see that she had been quite a challenging child and her father really had thought she didn't want those two old sausages.

The wise woman made the switcheroo for each of the family members. As soon as they could see from the other's perspective, they understood each other much better and their hearts softened. When everyone was back in their own bodies, the wise woman invited them to forgive each other.

She asked them to hold hands and say to each other, "Even though I don't agree with what you did, and even though I may not ever understand it, I refuse to carry any ill will against you for a moment longer. I completely, utterly and thoroughly free myself of my resentment. I free you and forgive you absolutely, body, heart and soul."

Intuitively, the eldest daughter knew what to do next. She scooped up those first two ancient sausages from her pile, and threw them into the open fire. She watched until the fire had completely burned them away. Then she walked up to her father and hugged him.

Following her lead, each family member gathered a handful of their mouldering offerings and threw their resentment into the fire. They hugged each other whilst the fire burned everything away.

The wise woman clapped her hands together and the rest of the mouldering pile of resentments shot up into the air like a swarm of insects and flew over the heads of the family into the flames. They burnt up and were gone. Everyone breathed a huge sigh of relief.

They all thanked their very special guest deeply and sincerely. Mother opened a window to let in some fresh air and the wise woman removed the wooden peg from her nose and slipped it back into her bag. After she did this, the Christmas table instantly replenished itself with the most delicious Christmas dinner any of them had ever seen, including plenty of mini sausages.

They all settled back in their places around the festive table. The father picked up the expensive-looking cracker by his plate and offered the other end of it to his eldest daughter. She gracefully took it. Everyone crossed arms, holding a cracker in each hand, and in one big circle counted down "Three, two, one!" and pulled. "Merry Christmas, everyone!"

EVEN EASIER

You might be surprised by what miracles can happen on the other side of your forgiveness work. My clients frequently describe feeling lighter, sometimes transformed, with subtly, noticeably or even hugely improved relationships and sometimes experience the reconciliation of their whole family, like Sarah did after she forgave her father. They report improvements in their health and progress in their careers and say things like, "You didn't just change my life, you saved it".

Ultimately, forgiveness – refusing to hold onto your ill will – is your choice. I'm not saying you *should* forgive. But given what you now know about what a racket resentment is, and what your ego is up to, why *wouldn't* you forgive? It takes more effort to hold on to resentment than to let it go. That's how forgiveness becomes 'easy'. You see through the ego and realise you can't escape experiencing all of the side-effects of resentment. Forgiveness then becomes the obvious choice. The process itself is simple. All you're really doing is having a powerful, authentic, imaginary conversation with someone, out loud.

GETTING UNSTUCK

But even when you sincerely want to forgive there can be places where you might get stuck in your forgiveness process - even before you start. I'm going to show you what to look out for. I'm also going to share a couple of quick techniques you can use when you know you're starting to feel resentful and you want to try to let go of it now rather than later. This is like dealing with the sausages one at a time rather than waiting for a wall to pile up.

If you practice forgiving the little things, it makes it easier to let go of bigger, more significant things when they come along.

I'll also talk about the practice of self-forgiveness. Sometimes the biggest resentment we hold is against ourselves. Forgiving yourself can be the most challenging, and also, the most liberating, forgiveness work you can do.

WHAT TO DO IF YOU GET STUCK

Don't underestimate the ego's resistance to the whole idea of forgiveness. If you're following the steps, and you've tried to forgive, but you're still feeling lingering resentment or are unwilling to let go, here are some things to try:

- ✓ Remind yourself of the true meaning of forgiveness. It is, *"The absolute refusal to hold ill will against someone for something they did or didn't do."*

- ✓ Remember that you are forgiving the *person, and* not condoning their behaviour. If you feel uncomfortable with the idea of 'judging' someone's behaviour, you can reframe it as 'discernment'. As William Ury suggests, "Be soft on the person, hard on the issue."

✓ Remind yourself who you're doing the process for. *You* are the one you're setting free. Even though others may also benefit - and the world will too - forgiveness is for your heart, your peace of mind, your wellbeing.

✓ Check in with your body to make sure you have said *everything* that needs to be said *out loud*. The words need to be spoken. Don't try to be polite, or politically or spiritually correct, or censor anything. Be real. If you are working on something from your childhood or early life, you can imagine a younger version of yourself speaking first. This can be very healing especially if the younger you didn't express themselves fully at the time.

✓ Give yourself all the time you need. I worked with one woman with a violently abusive mother and it took us over an hour to do just the heart to heart part of the process where she was confessing all of her resentment. It's very unlikely you will need to take anywhere near as long! You don't need to repeat yourself. If you use the prompts like "I resent you for all the times when....", this can cover more ground efficiently. The most important thing is to express the *full* extent of your resentment and say what needs to be said.

✓ Make sure you step completely into the other person's shoes and look out through their eyes, even if it feels uncomfortable to do this. You can also ask yourself if there would be any circumstances under which you might have done a similar thing. In his book *"The Wisdom of Forgiveness"*, the Dalai Lama reveals the circumstances under which even he could imagine committing an act of violence. Stay humble about your own ego too. We all have one. If this part is too challenging for you to do by yourself and you're feeling a lot of fear or resistance, or it doesn't feel safe, then get support.

✓ If you're having trouble with going higher, or you're hearing the other person say only defensive and unhelpful things, you can try imagining them as a young child or a baby. Sometimes this helps to evoke your compassion and empathy.

✓ It can be really hard to let go of something if you don't know why you're holding on to it. Often, the goodies that you're getting out of holding on to your resentment are so subtle or familiar, they're hard to spot. That's why you need to shift to the balcony and take a higher perspective so that you can hear your inner dialogue and observe your ego. Check out the list of payoffs in chapter six and be willing to get really honest with yourself about the games your ego is playing. Then try this step again.

✓ Be honest about what carrying your resentment is costing you. When I'm working in person with a client and they're not connecting with the true cost of carrying their resentment, I use the 'sofa cushion of resentment' technique. Whilst sitting under the weight of their resentment sofa-cushion, they get a visceral experience of the heavy and cumbersome burden they're carrying.

I once had to work with a client over two sessions because he didn't feel ready to let go of his resentment by the end of our first session. I left him with the sofa cushion on his lap and invited him to keep the cushion with him until the next day. He told me that it was while sitting underneath the weight of it, watching TV later that evening, feeling trapped, that he made the decision to set himself free. He also recognised there was more he needed to say to his mother, things that he wanted her to know before he could forgive her. We continued the next day and he successfully completed his process, with great relief.

You could try this experiment safely for yourself. Imagine sitting underneath your enormous sofa cushion of resentment while you're at work, watching TV, out with friends, cooking in your kitchen, exercising, making love and so on. It can also be helpful to write down your payoffs and costs in two lists and compare them. Then review your list again, to see how each of the goodies is also, ultimately, part of the cost. For example, the feeling of power your resentment gives you will be costing you your *actual* power to make a new choice, as well as costing you peace of mind.

✓ Sometimes, *you* may be the one who needs to be forgiven. There may be things you need to say to the other person about your own behaviour. Things you did that you need to own up to and take responsibility for. An 'effective apology', according to research by Roy Lewicki, includes several elements in order of importance:

1. Taking responsibility
2. Offering amends
3. Expressing regret
4. Explanation
5. Repentance
6. Requesting forgiveness

The research also shows that *how* you offer your apology matters - face to face is best. In the forgiveness process, it is an imaginary conversation but you may also wish to apologise in 'real life' if it's appropriate and safe to do so. It also helps to have the right tone of voice, be sincere, show that you care and that it matters to you.

The most important thing is the acknowledgement of responsibility. You may also wish to offer some kind of amends and express your regret. You can explain any extenuating circumstances (without making excuses), promise that it won't happen again and make a commitment to a new behaviour or attitude.

Probably the most important thing to remember is that forgiveness is *your* choice. No one can make you do it. You can nurture your resentments and take them all to your grave - even pass them on to your children if you wish - but why would you when you can choose freedom and peace of mind instead?

LETTING GO QUICKLY – THE SEDONA METHOD

There's a wonderful quick release method you can use when you need to forgive something relatively minor called the Sedona Method. It's a technique that helps you to notice and let go of any feeling or belief you are experiencing in the moment, regardless of how long you may have been holding onto it.

As soon as you notice you are feeling resentful, or you catch your heart start to close, take a couple of deep breaths. You may feel physical sensations like tension or pain in your body. You may feel emotions like anger or indignation. You may have the urge to raise your voice, back down or run away.

Feel into the feeling, noticing where it is in your body. Then put your full attention on the feeling, breathe into it and ask yourself these questions:

-    "Could I allow myself to welcome this feeling?" –
     "Have this feeling?"

Then take another couple of deep breaths and ask yourself,

- "Could I allow myself to let this go?"
- "Would I let this go?"
- "When?"

Then you make your choice. You don't have to let it go. The choice is *always* yours.

The practice exercise they teach in the Sedona Method is to hold a pen or pencil tightly in your hand, gripping it until it begins to feel uncomfortable. Then, when you're ready, simply turn your hand over, palm facing down, open your fingers, and the pen falls out. This is how you imagine letting go of whatever issue or feeling is bothering you at the time.

The Sedona Method is wonderful for all the minor grievances that otherwise gather like little stones in your shoes, but I've never seen it work for significant accumulations of resentment without a lot of preliminary work beforehand. And if you're in the full throes of rage you'll most likely need to wait for the wave to pass and give yourself time to distance yourself from your ego.

You can also use practices like Emotional Freedom Technique (EFT, also known as 'Tapping') when you notice you've been triggered and are feeling in pain (including physical pain). EFT helps to safely meet and release strong emotions using a combination of Chinese acupressure points and Western psychology. If a client has experienced physical trauma as part of what they're working to forgive, I'll include EFT in their process. For more information on this technique, please see the resources section at the back of the book.

The Sedona Method and EFT require you to notice that you've been triggered and sometimes that doesn't happen immediately. If you use either of these approaches and they don't work for you, then just add the person you're resenting to your list and make time to do your forgiveness work later on.

THOUGHTS VS FEELINGS

Feelings are physical, they're experienced in the body. Thoughts are in your mind, yet they can be so powerful they physically affect the body. Just try this little experiment:

Imagine a huge, ripe, juicy lemon. Feel the weight of it in your hand and the texture of the skin. Then imagine slowly cutting it in half with a sharp knife and watch the juices dribbling onto the chopping board. Bring one of the halves up to your nose and smell the lemony fragrance. Then reach out your tongue and lick the whole of the cut side. Feel the difference in the textures between the flesh and the pith as you taste the sour sharpness of the juice... Most likely, you'll be feeling some kind of response in your salivary glands – and that's just with an *imaginary lemon*!

You can learn to notice your body's physiological responses when something happens that triggers strong feelings in you. Developing your sensitivity to the flow of sensations and emotions in your body can increase your emotional intelligence and resilience. Becoming aware of how it feels in your body when you hold resentment helps you notice when you have an un-met expectation or script running for the other person. You can go through the doorway of your feelings to discover your ego's deepest fears and beliefs.

The difference between a thought and a feeling is that your thoughts are your lightning-quick (usually unconscious) interpretation of events. Your feelings are your chemical, physiological response to those thoughts. Of course, you can have feelings that are directly caused by physical stimuli (e.g. the sight of blood), but when it comes to relationships and your reactive behaviour, your feelings will be caused by your unconscious thoughts and beliefs.

When I *believe* I've been rejected, because you don't want to come round for supper on Tuesday, I might *feel* anger, sadness, jealousy or disappointment, depending on what reason I think is behind your 'rejection'. It's the *meaning* I'm giving the situation that's causing my upset and my feelings. I could just as easily be delighted that you're not coming round on Tuesday because it means I can catch up on some important paperwork or go out dancing instead.

LETTING GO QUICKLY – INNER DIALOGUE VERSION

If I take the time to question the meaning I'm making and ask myself, "Is it true, false or don't know that I've been rejected?" I can discover the objective truth, e.g. you have your volleyball class end of term party this Tuesday. I haven't been rejected. You're just busy. And I have other options I can choose as well.

When it comes to other people it can be a great relief to keep a beginner's mind about your version of reality and say, simply, "I don't know". This feels scary for your ego because it loves to know. That's part of how it keeps itself safe. But you *don't* know what's motivating someone else's behaviour or what they're really thinking - most of the time you're drawing conclusions that simply aren't verifiably true. You probably don't know the full story and you might be misinterpreting, making assumptions, missing important information or projecting onto someone. If you're in any doubt, just ask yourself, "How can I *know* that this is true?" (as in Byron Katie's process, *The Work*).

Questioning what you believe is one of the most powerful transformational techniques that I know, along with forgiveness and meditation. Becoming aware of your ego's scripts and biased world view, and questioning any meaning you're making, can be of great help in practicing authentic forgiveness. As soon as you notice you're feeling anything uncomfortable that makes you want to withdraw or close your heart, it's likely you've made an interpretation of events that has disturbed your ego. You can then enquire within. This can act like a preventative measure against harbouring resentment, because if I'm able to question my ego's beliefs about having been 'rejected' and find it's not true, I won't be holding any grievance against you when you call to re-arrange our meeting.

The more you're aware of the expectations, demands and reactivity of your ego, the less resentment you'll gather.

SELF-FORGIVENESS

Self-forgiveness can often be the most challenging forgiveness practice of all. There are several reasons for this;

1. It's hard to be objective about yourself.

2. Some of your oldest habitual ways of thinking will be so embedded that these beliefs will 'feel' as if they're part of you – or even as if they *are* you. Just to reassure you, every person I've ever worked with has at least one strongly held negative belief about themselves. Usually there's a whole collection of negative self-beliefs lurking at the bottom of our ego structure which is why we're so afraid to be vulnerable - to avoid them being exposed.

3. The need for self-forgiveness doesn't feel quite the same as when you're holding resentment against someone else. You might not recognize it, either. It's often experienced as being harshly judgemental of yourself, making yourself wrong or even subtly punishing yourself. Often resentment against yourself feels very current and alive, even when what you think you need to forgive happened a long time ago.

4. You might feel vulnerable as you experience your pain, shame or regret, and want to avoid these feelings. But just gently allow yourself to feel whatever arises, exactly as you do when you're working on forgiving someone else.

5. You might need to face things about yourself you would rather deny or avoid and have pushed out of your awareness for a long time.

6. Sometimes you might even feel resentful towards yourself for what you like or appreciate about yourself. As the famous Marianne Williamson quote from *A Return to Love* goes, "Our deepest fear is not that we are inadequate, our deepest fear is that we are powerful beyond measure." Your ego may be resistant to facing what's good in you and your phenomenal potential because of fear, pride, vanity and unrealistic expectations (yours and everyone else's).

7. You might be afraid that if you forgive yourself, you'll no longer have the incentive to change in the ways you want. But this kind of ego-led thinking is obviously false – you are always free to be loving and encouraging towards yourself as you make changes in your life. Resenting yourself won't help. Loving yourself better, will.

You can do your self-forgiveness practice in two ways. One is with a regular Forgiveness Made Easy process. Bring an image of your current or younger self to your forgiveness chair - particularly if there was a time in your life when you did something that you now regret. Then follow the steps of the process.

The other alternative is to do the process facing a mirror. The first time I did this, I felt terrified to face myself in this way. However, it can be incredibly powerful and transformational, and well worth the investment of your time. Please see the resources section if you're interested in knowing more.

BYPASS THE SPIRITUAL BYPASS

One other potential place where you might get stuck is if you have particular beliefs, most likely spiritual ones, that make it hard for you to judge another person's behaviour or admit you're carrying any resentment.

Or you might believe there's nothing to forgive because nothing really happened - reality is just 'illusion' or 'maya'. This is what Ken Wilber would call a 'category error'. For the purposes of the process,

I encourage you to honour your life's experience. Don't try to deny or condone any kind of abuse, trauma or unacceptable behaviour by 'not judging' or trying to do some kind of spiritual bypass on it.

The ego likes to have a reason to explain why something out of its control has happened. This 'spiritual' answer can feel less intolerable to the ego than surrendering and admitting it may never understand the mysteries of existence or why anything happens, good or bad.

I would never suggest to anyone who's been abused, raped or neglected that they 'chose' to have that experience happen to them. You may have experienced things, physically or emotionally, that were traumatic, and the Forgiveness Made Easy process includes, integrates and honours that.

Even if you're able to find a way to derive positive meaning from your experience because your faith allows you to see grace even in the darkest of circumstances, do the process anyway. Even if you have learned profound life lessons from your experience, you will still benefit from doing your forgiveness practice.

During your process, keep your heart open and be as compassionate as you can about the events of the past, both towards yourself and any others who were involved. If you suffered at the time, or since, honour that. It's important to do your forgiveness work authentically, including your suffering, your pain and all your feelings.

PRACTICE, PRACTICE, PRACTICE

Just like any other skill or technique, your ability to let go of your resentment will improve the more you practice doing it. Brad Brown used to say, "Practice, practice, practice until it becomes your practice."

Often relationships are complex and the willingness to forgive may uncover layers that have built up over time. Just go as deep as you can and trust that you will be able to face whatever it is that your psyche shows you each time. I believe that the psyche is self-healing, and just like your body, is able to heal itself given the right conditions. The important thing is to be willing to do your work every time you notice you're triggered or that you're accumulating ill will. Have an intention to notice the little stones in your shoes, before they start giving you blisters. Notice when you begin to hobble a little and tip those stones out! Notice and let go, notice and let go.

There's an old saying that goes, "If you're too busy to meditate, you're too busy." I feel the same way about forgiveness. It's always going to be worth your time and effort. Resentment back guarantee!

PREVENTION IS BETTER THAN CURE

To me, forgiveness is like a forgotten or latent superpower that's ready for us to use at any time - we just have to access it. I'm amazed and inspired by how willing people are to forgive once they understand what's been in their way and how much they've been suffering by holding on to their resentment. We human beings have this capacity as part of our nature. We are social creatures and, "our capacity for forgiveness is every bit as authentic as our capacity for revenge." (from Michael E McCulloch's *Beyond Revenge – the Evolution of the Forgiveness Instinct*.)

Evolutionary spirituality teacher, Andrew Cohen, used the phrase, "living a life of constant resolution", to mean you consciously clear up any misunderstandings or issues in your relationships as soon as possible so that there is nothing 'out' between you and someone else. You're not still chewing over what happened last Wednesday, wishing you'd said something, stood up for yourself or asked about what happened.

Living a life of constant resolution is a high ideal, and yet it is possible if you are willing to be radically honest and practice forgiveness often, along with clear, non-violent communication.

FREEDOM FROM THE PAST

Whatever you believe about the past, you can choose not to let it affect your present experience or your future. You are completely in charge of this dynamic, even if there have been physical consequences, e.g. injury or trauma that were beyond your control. You are always responsible for how you meet and respond to the situations in your life and the meaning you derive from them. That's where your power is.

Imagine how amazing you'd feel if all of the energy that's tied up in holding on to any resentment gets released into your life and fuels the things you really value like your creativity, your health, your business, your love life or taking care of our planet.

When you do your forgiveness work you're not just setting up new neural pathways in your own brain, you're changing the collective unconscious. In the last chapter, I'll outline why I believe we need a forgiveness revolution and what's in it for the world.

Practice Suggestion: If you do get stuck in your process, try any of these recommendations. If you discover something that works particularly well for you and want to pass on the tip, please let me know so I can share it with others!

CHAPTER ELEVEN
THE FUTURE POTENTIAL

"Nothing that I can do will change the structure of the universe.
But maybe, by raising my voice,
I can help in the greatest of all causes –
Good will among men and peace on earth."

Albert Einstein

I hope that you feel inspired to do your forgiveness practice often and transform your relationships and your life. I also want to encourage you to appreciate how much the contribution of your peaceful heart matters to the world. What really inspired me to write this book is the phenomenal potential that forgiveness has to bring us closer towards a world at peace. We're all interconnected and it matters to the whole of humanity, and maybe to life itself, that we each do our forgiveness work.

When I was growing up in the UK, there was a TV programme my whole family loved to watch called *Tomorrow's World* about new technologies and trends for the future. Back then, the future seemed exciting and full of potential. Now, if you talk to people about their vision of the future it's usually pretty dark.

We need a new, audacious vision for an inspiring, abundant, peaceful future. As William Ury, says, "We know how to end hunger, how to prevent war, and how to use clean energy to save the environment. The central obstacle in the way is us. It is our difficulty in coming together to cooperate. In order to build a better, safer and healthier world for ourselves and for our children, we must be able to deal with our differences constructively and creatively."

We will never be able to do this without both the ability to forgive and a vision of how the world can be transformed by forgiveness.

I've always been inspired by Brad Brown's vision for the world. His vision was that the simple mental health and emotional intelligence tools that he taught would be used by everyone on an everyday basis, "just like brushing your teeth". They'd be taught by parents and carers and be integrated in every school, university, business and place of worship, and would be reflected in our culture, arts, technology and commerce practices. Everyone would know about their inner dialogue and how to question their assumptions and beliefs. Everyone would know how to authentically and profoundly forgive, and be practicing forgiveness frequently in their everyday lives.

We're social creatures and we adopt behaviours that we learn from others. We're more motivated by what our neighbours do than by financial incentives. You're more likely to do your recycling, or conserve rain water, if you know all your neighbours are doing it. Our brains sync up when we witness each other's behaviours. Our mirror neurons fire and we receive pleasure just by witnessing acts of kindness towards others.

This means that what you do matters more than you may realise. It matters not just to you and your immediate circle, but to all of us. Imagine you can pinch a tiny section of the universe (a bit like a piece of fabric), and raise it up... the rest of the fabric will move too. The nearest parts to where you're pinching will get lifted up the most, but even the furthest edges will be moved.

This is how your forgiveness practice will help to change the world:

1. You learn how to do a simple, profound, forgiveness process.
2. You do the process frequently, and your behaviour changes.
3. The practice changes your relationships with the people you forgive and how you show up in your life. This impacts human culture from the inside out.
4. When culture changes, the structures of society will also change (i.e. potential global disarmament).

Four steps to global peace! How long do you think it would take you to forgive everyone you needed to in your life? If you took a day off and did nothing else but focus on forgiveness, could you do it in a day? Even if you've been harbouring a lot of grudges and you're busy juggling all the different demands of your life, you could probably still get through everyone and everything you need to forgive in a week or possibly two.

A couple of weeks to peace - in your heart at least. And that's probably true of every individual. Imagine how it would be for you to let go of all your resentment, person by person, thing by thing. You forgive everyone you're in relationship with, you forgive yourself, you forgive your body, the way you eat, you forgive your neighbourhood, your politicians, your country, your pet (if you have one), your disease (if you have one), your god (if you have one) – everyone and everything until you declare your heart a garden of peace.

Imagine the depth of release in the weeks to come. Peace in your family. Peace in your office. Peace in your school. Peace in your community. How about if everyone did the same? If everyone, in those same couple of weeks, did their forgiveness work?

I hope you can see the amazing potential that I can see.

I believe forgiveness is one of the highest expressions of love and that it's both an evolutionary and a revolutionary act. I don't know of any other single choice we each could make that would have such a far-reaching, transformational effect on the whole of humanity.

Now you know how forgiveness can be made easy, I hope you'll join me and practice forgiveness often in your everyday life. I also hope you'll be inspired to share your experience of the transformational power of this simple practice with others. If you have a story to share, please post it on our page: *www.facebook.com/ForgivenessMadeEasy*

Forgiveness is the laying down of arms and defences. When you put aside your personal weapons and surrender the shield over your heart, your forgiveness becomes an act of amnesty for humanity.

Together, we can be the (r)evolution of peace.

Practice Suggestion: *I hope you will feel inspired to practice the Forgiveness Made Easy process any time you need it. If you'd like a free recording of me taking you step-by-step through the process, you can download it here:*

www.forgivenessmadeeasy.co.uk/bookbonus

"To forgive is to set a prisoner free
and to discover
that the prisoner was you."

Lewis B Smedes

ACKNOWLEDGEMENTS

Firstly, I'd like to extend an enormous thank you to all of my amazing crowdfunding sponsors who so generously supported the writing of this book. Thank you for your kind words of encouragement and belief in me, for seeing the value in this subject, and entrusting me with your faith and with your cash:

Christian Vydelingum, Adrian Wood, Anonymous, Earl 'Raj' Purdy, Jim Pope, David Templer, Taylor Madison Damion, Jenny Andrew, David Harris, Annie Sherborne, Jenny Dowling, Annette Kenney, Fiona Collinson, Anonymous, David Templer (again!), Anonymous, Volosity Freefly, Linda Kay, Noomi Melchoir Natan, Chris Vickers, Kate, Marian Canvin, Anonymous, Shauna Scales, Angela Halverson Bogo, Jennifer de Brye, Debbie Prime, Philip Lawson, Fiona Milligan, Michaela O'Driscoll, Ekkehard Weisner, Emma & Marty Rose, Susan, Rod Dueck, Cornelia Durrant, Rick Bissonette, Helen Buckley, Mosipoos, Joanna Seere, Vivien De Bernardi, Ann, Andreas Prohl, Alan Chapman, Thomas Ward, Nick Bowles/Doug Stone, Anonymous, Sarah Van Gelder, Melanie Menell, Catherine Butler, Phil Simpson, Sue & Mark Wade, Sue Whiting, Craig Hamilton, Erica Mae Yonge, Sara Vian, Denise Sparrow, Ian Flooks, Ollie Gibb, Annie Lionnet, Linda Lubin, Jotipal Kaur, Eva Pundyk and Helen Pearley.

To all my Anonymous donors – I especially thank you because I can't thank you in person - I don't know who you are!

I also want to particularly acknowledge Ian Flooks whose generosity, not just this time, but many times in my life has made all the difference to both the view from my window and whether or not my creative output makes it into the world.

To my friend Taylor without whose timely love, encouragement and support, I might have baulked at the daunting tasks of crowd-funding and writing this book. Thank you for all of your creative and supportive input, your fabulous cover design, your make-over and presentation suggestions, your video and interviewing skills and for being the creative genius and inspiration that you are.

Thank you to Jared Meuser for permission to use your fantastic artwork on my cover – your profound image is a perfect expression of how we have the power to relieve ourselves of so much of our own self-perpetuated suffering!

I also hugely acknowledge, appreciate and make a deep bow of thanks to all my private clients - especially those of you who have been working with me long-term; committed and dedicated to the adventure of your own evolution. In particular – a special thank you to Sarah and also to Debra and Hazel for offering your stories. You are an inspiration. Thank you all for everything I've learned through working with each and every one of you as you've helped me to shape my understanding of the depths of the human heart as it encounters the opportunity to forgive and evolve. Thank you for trusting me and for giving me permission to use your inspirational anecdotes in this book. It is a privilege and a pleasure to serve you. You are all amazing beings!

I am also so grateful for the interest, generosity and support for this book from so many of our fabulous Vital Detox clients. Thank you for giving me permission to share some of your stories too, and for your courage, willingness and trust. Every retreat we are inspired and evoked by you, and grateful for the opportunity to repeatedly witness the transformational potential of forgiveness.

Special and enormous thanks also go to Fiona Milligan and Rachel Carr Hill for helping me to develop my experience and understanding of the art of forgiveness by practicing with me regularly over many years, and in addition to my phenomenal evolutionary friend, Melanie Menell, for almost two decades of support through my own life process. Extra enormous thanks.

A gigantic thank you to Annie Lionnet for your enthusiastic encouragement and support for my vision from the very beginning, for being my role model and inspiration and for all your generous advice on the significant timings of my marketing efforts.

I'd like to extend an enormous thank you to my Vital Detox 'family' – it's a privilege to be part of such a transformational offering to the world and to be practicing the living art of forgiveness working alongside you all. An eternal and effulgent thank you to each of you - especially to founder Anna Tolson for your bold and beautiful creation and for having the brilliance to draw the phenomenal team of Annie, Fi, Fran, Andrew, Rachel, Angeliki and Tony together. Looking forward to the next episode!

I dip a grateful curtsy of thanks and heartfelt appreciation to my passionate, straight-talking book coach and mentor, Angela Lauria – thank you for those first nine weeks of inspiration and encouragement in getting this book out of the petri dish and into the incubator.

I also want to heartily acknowledge and thank my editorial team of volunteers: Rodney Dueck, Simon Hunt, Rachel Carr-Hill, Jonathan Halliwell, Francesca Creffield, Ian Flooks and Ollie Gibb. Your thoughtful, intelligent and encouraging feedback throughout the process was absolutely invaluable.

In particular, I want to extend yet another enormous and endless thank you to my copy editor and proof-reader, Fiona Milligan - it was a privilege and honour to have your experienced 'policeman's' eyes as well as your compassionate heart focussed on my final draft.

Thank you, thank you, thank you to every one of my early readers and book launch team members. Thank you for your patience through the editing process and for your generous interest and enthusiasm for this book. Thank you for your warm words of encouragement and reflection, for spreading the word and for helping to create global peace, one heart at a time.

I'm grateful to all of my sounding boards for your invaluable feedback – and particularly to Alan Chapman for your encouraging and thoughtful suggestions for the marketing and promoting of this book.

I also want to acknowledge all of my spiritual and personal development teachers, without whose work, inspiration and guidance, I wouldn't be who I am today. In particular, Craig Hamilton – thank you for all you are - you are my evolutionary inspiration and role model – a living exemplar of everything you teach.

I am forever indebted to and deeply thank the late K Bradford Brown and W Roy Whitten for the profound teachings of the More to Life programme and the cumulative effect of living the heart of those teachings for over two decades. Daily, your legacy continues to help me dance on the moving carpet of life!

And I sincerely thank Brandon Bays for the framework of *The Journey*, you've birthed an inspired, unique and transformational process. Your work harnesses the healing powers of the psyche in a truly extraordinary way.

I also hugely acknowledge leadership genius Jonathan Wolf Phillips for never giving up on me and for continuing to support my accountability and awareness of what's most important in the short, medium and long term!

I am deeply grateful to Ken Wilber, Marianne Williamson, Gabrielle Roth, Nigel Wali Hamilton, Thomas Huebl, Brian Swimme, Alison Armstrong, Eckhart Tolle, Earl 'Raj' Purdy, Neale Donald Walsch, Anthony Robbins, Deepak Chopra, Jayem and Andrew Cohen, all of whose work and teachings are woven into a life-enhancing tapestry that continues to profoundly source my evolutionary adventure.

I'd also like to honour those spiritual masters who have inspired me with their lives, their teachings, their science or their art – The Dalai Lama, Albert Einstein, Hafiz, Kahlil Gibran, Rumi, Pema Chodron, Stevie Wonder, Rudolph Steiner, Leonard Cohen, Richard Bach, Michael A. Singer, each one of you lives in my heart.

I also extend an enormous thank you to all my friends, family (especially my supportive, creative, and extraordinary siblings, Maria and Simon), my practice circle partners, triad, evolutionary and spiritual community members who encourage me, source me, believe in me and enrich my life in all the myriad ways that you do. I extend heartfelt thanks to Earl Purdy, for teaching me the art of appreciation and for championing all of my creative and spiritual pursuits. And an extra-large helping of gratitude goes to Will Angeloro for recording the audio for the Forgiveness Made Easy Process.

I deeply and inadequately bow in eternal gratitude to my amazing, wise, brilliant, publicity shy editor (who requested to remain anonymous) for skillfully pruning my manuscript into a coherent, authentic whole. Your insight, patience, humour and clarity have blessed and transformed this book beyond measure. Thank you for seeing this book's potential and for honouring our vision through every draft.

Thank you to my darling son, Ollie, for bringing so much joy and laughter into my life, but also for giving me such sage and encouraging feedback, for being chief cook and bottle washer, and for working so hard alongside me to help get this book out into the world... Forgiveness Made Easy is for you and the generations to come - may you all be part of a truly inspiring future.

To everyone, including those I might have inadvertently forgotten – thank you, thank you, thank you. Here's to the evolution of peace in our lifetime.

In loving memory of my parents John & Christine Hunt

"To err is human; to forgive, divine."

Alexander Pope

NOTES

INTRODUCTION

"Forgiveness is mental, emotional..." An article linking gum disease to heart disease can be found here: http://www.nhs.uk/Livewell/dentalhealth/Pages/gum-disease-and-overall-health.aspx

CHAPTER 1

"Forgiveness is..." definition from K Bradford Brown, founder of the 'More to Life' program: http://moretolife.org.uk/
"As I walked out..." from Nelson Mandela's Autobiography: Mandela, N (1995). *Long Walk to Freedom: the autobiography of Nelson Mandela*. 2nd ed. London: Abacus.
"Forgiveness is not opposed..." from an interview with Archbishop Desmond Tutu: http://www.beliefnet.com/wellness/2001/10/are-we-ready-to-forgive.aspx
"For example, Azim Khamisa's..." the Tariq Khamisa Foundation website is: https://tkf.org/
"The need to forgive is widely..." from the 'Forgiveness' Wikipedia page: https://en.wikipedia.org/wiki/Forgiveness

CHAPTER 2

"When psychiatrist/psychotherapist..." Gerry Jampolsky's website can be found here: http://www.ahinternational.org/about/about-ahinternational/about-the-ahi-team

"See Katherine Woodward Thomas'…" Woodward Thomas, K (2015). *Conscious Uncoupling: The 5 Steps to Living Happily Even After.* New York: Random House. For further information see the Conscious Uncoupling website:
http://www.consciousuncoupling.com

"In his article, *The Complicated…"* the article can be found here:
https://www.scribd.com/document/335636803/The-Complicated-Psychology-of-Revenge-Association-for-Psychological-Science

"In *Beyond Revenge…"* McCullough, M (2008). *Beyond Revenge.* San Francisco: Jossey-Bass. For further information, check out:
http://www.beyondrevengebook.com/

"Dr.Wilson says…" the study referenced can be found here:
http://www.drlwilson.com/ARTICLES/FORGIVING.htm

"Latest reports show…." the study referenced can be found here:
http://www.huffingtonpost.com/joe-robinson/stress-and-health_b_3313606.html

"Negative affect and chronic…" this study can be found here:
http://journal.frontiersin.org/article/10.3389/fnhum.2013.00839/full

"Negotiation expert…" Ury, W (2015). *Getting to Yes with Yourself: (and Other Worthy Opponents).* New York: Harper Collins. For further info, check out his website: http://www.williamury.com

"Dr. Christiane Northrup…" Northrup, C (2001). *The Wisdom of Menopause: Creating Physical and Emotional Health During the Change.* London: Piatkus Books. For further information:
http://www.drnorthrup.com/wisdom-of-menopause/

CHAPTER 3

"In the famous 'Selective Attention' …" the video can be found here: https://www.youtube.com/watch?v=vJG698U2Mvo

"In Professor Steve Peter's…" Peters, S (2012). *The Chimp Paradox: The Mind Management Programme to Help You Achieve Success, Confidence and Happiness*. UK: Vermillion: http://chimpmanagement.com/the-chimp-model/the-book/

"This isn't to say that…" Masters, R (2010). *Spiritual Bypassing*. California: North Atlantic Books. For more information, see the website: http://robertmasters.com/book/spiritual-bypassing

"Viktor Frankl knew…" attributed to Viktor E Frankl: Austrian neurologist and Psychiatrist (1905 - 1997). See also book list in resources section and for further information about his life and work, visit: http://www.viktorfrankl.org/e/lifeandwork.html

CHAPTER 4

"In Brené Brown's…" Brown, B (2012). *Daring Greatly*. USA: Gotham Books. For more, see her website: http://Brenébrown.com/

"The power of the powerless…" attributed to K Bradford Brown, of the 'More to Life' program: http://moretolife.org.uk/

"It's also a process…" this quote's source can be found here: http://theforgivenessproject.com/stories/desmond-tutu-south-africa/

"Known as ACEs in…" Jackson Nakazawa, D (2015). *Childhood Disrupted: How Your Biography Becomes Your Biology, and How You Can Heal*. New York: Simon and Schuster.: https://donnajacksonnakazawa.com/childhood-disrupted/

"As Khalil Gibran…" Gibran, K (1997). *the Prophet*. Middlesex: Tiger Books. For more information on his life and work, see: https://en.wikipedia.org/wiki/Kahlil_Gibran

"If you're interested to…" Bolte Taylor, J (2009). *My Stroke of Insight*. London: Hodder and Stoughton. For more information, see: http://www.mystrokeofinsight.com/ and for her inspirational TED

talk:
https://www.ted.com/talks/jill_bolte_taylor_s_powerful_stroke_of_insight

CHAPTER 5

"In *The Untethered Soul...*" Singer, M (2007). *the Untethered Soul*. USA: New Harbinger Publications Inc. For further information, see: http://untetheredsoul.com/

"Whether you believe..." attributed to Henry Ford: American industrialist and founder of the Ford Motor Company (1863 - 1947)

"In J P Carse's..." Carse, J (1995). *Breakfast at the Victory*. USA: Harper Collins.

"In David Allen's..." Allen, D (2001). *Getting Things Done*. Cornwall: Piatkus Books. For more information: http://gettingthingsdone.com/

"I then ask myself..." attributed to K Bradford Brown, of the *More to Life* program: http://moretolife.org.uk/

CHAPTER 6

"I definitely felt..." find out more about the More to Life program here: http://moretolife.org.uk/about-our-courses/weekend/

"Jack Canfield, who..." hear Jack Canfield talking about Catherine Lanigan here: https://www.youtube.com/watch?v=ft3UsMIM5Hg

"According to Michael..." McCullough, M (2008). *Beyond Revenge*. San Francisco: Jossey-Bass. For more information, see: http://www.beyondrevengebook.com/

"As Brené Brown..." Brené's website can be found here: http://Brenébrown.com/ Brown, B (2012). *Daring Greatly*. USA: Gotham Books.

CHAPTER 7

"As Bessel van der Kolk..." Levine, P (2015). *Trauma and Memory*. USA: North Atlantic Books.

"In Bruce Lipton's..." Lipton, B (2013). *the Honeymoon Effect*. London: Hay House. https://www.brucelipton.com/books/honeymoon-effect

"In another of Bruce..." Lipton, B (2015). *the Biology of Belief*. London: Hay House. See his website: https://www.brucelipton.com/

CHAPTER 8

"It does not matter how..." A Course in Miracles website can be found here: https://www.acim.org/. Also see resources section for more ACIM links.

"When you feel pain..." Singer, M (2007). *The Untethered Soul*. USA: New Harbinger Publications Inc. See: http://untetheredsoul.com/

"According to American..." the Ken Wilber Superhuman OS website can be found here: https://superhumanos.net/.

"In Stephen Covey's..." Covey, S (1989). *the Seven Habits of Highly Effective People*. London: Simon and Schuster. For more, see: https://www.stephencovey.com/7habits/7habits.php

"One of my spiritual..." Craig Hamilton's Integral Enlightenment website is: http://integralenlightenment.com/academy/

CHAPTER 9

"There's a very..." Blanton, B (2005). *Radical Honesty*. USA: Sparrowhawk Publications. For more information, see:

http://radicalhonesty.com/store/books/

"Otherwise it might…" a free PDF of Marshall Rosenburg's non-violent communication techniques can be downloaded from here: http://www.nonviolentcommunication.com/aboutnvc/4partproces s.htm. There are also links to a free YouTube of an NVC workshop and other materials in the resources section.

CHAPTER 10

"As William Ury…" William Ury's website can be found here: http://www.williamury.com/

"In his book the…" HH the Dalai Lama and Chan, V (2005). *the Wisdom of Forgiveness*. Kent: Hodder and Stoughton.

"An 'effective apology', according…" Roy Lewicki's paper on negotiation and conflict management can be found here: http://onlinelibrary.wiley.com/journal/10.1111/(ISSN)1750-4716

"There's a wonderful quick…" a link to the Sedona Method website can be found here: http://www.sedona.com/Home.asp

"How can I *know*…" Byron Katie's *'The Work'* website is: http://thework.com/en

"This is what Ken…" You may also be interested in other works by philosopher Ken Wilber: http://www.kenwilber.com

"Our capacity for…" McCullough, M (2008). *Beyond Revenge*. San Francisco: Jossey-Bass. See: http://www.beyondrevengebook.com/

"Evolutionary spiritual…" Andrew Cohen's website can be found here: http://www.andrewcohen.com/

RESOURCES

Listed below are a few extra resources for those of you who may wish to continue to explore your journey of forgiveness and your evolutionary potential in a variety of ways.

THERAPEUTIC SUPPORT

Wherever I have recommended that you seek professional help from a therapist, forgiveness coach or mentor who can support you with your process, please refer to your own therapist or coach, or look for a Journey therapist via *www.thejourney.com* or consider a mind-body- spirit retreat like *Vital Detox UK - www.vitaldetox.com*

TRAININGS

You can also engage in weekend or week-long personal/spiritual development trainings such as those offered by the *More to Life* organisation and in the USA, *More to Life US.* One of the most important elements of the *More to Life* weekend workshops is Brad Brown's teaching on forgiveness – which is reflected in my own approach.

I wholeheartedly recommend all of the on-line courses by Integral Enlightenment teacher, Craig Hamilton. If you are serious about evolving beyond your ego, check out his essential 9-week *Integral Enlightenment Course - Awakening to an Evolutionary Relationship to Life.*

Another core influence on my work is *The Journey* by Brandon Bays. *The Journey Intensive* - is a weekend introduction to Journey work. Both her book, *The Journey* and her courses include forgiveness as a key element of the process.

I also recommend Byron Katie's *The Work* as part of how you get free of your mind's interpretations of the past - both her live and on-line talks and workshops. There are free resources and worksheets on her website.

The other kind of therapeutic work I highly respect and recommend is *Family Constellation* work, founded by Bert Hellinger. It can be an extraordinary supplement to forgiveness. It's like a live, 3-D version of the imaginary work you can do in your heart, seeing the family or any group system as a whole - from multiple perspectives.

TECHNIQUES

Meditation is probably the most effective foundational practice that will enhance your whole life in general. It can help you establish and maintain inner equilibrium and develop your ability to stay present even in the face of challenging circumstances as well as be able to let go more easily. There are many kinds of meditation and mindfulness techniques, but my personal practice is the *Practice of Direct Awakening* taught by Craig Hamilton, who also offers free on-line monthly meditation gatherings, *Meditation for Evolutionaries.*

You can also explore practices that help to release trauma and stuck emotions from the body, like the Emotional Freedom Technique (EFT, also known as 'Tapping'). There are two main websites I recommend - Nick and Jessica Ortner's *The Tapping Solution.com* and

EFT Universe. Nick and Jessica host a free Tapping Summit every year which is both fascinating and an incredible free resource. You can learn more about tapping in general (it's fantastic for stage-fright, stress, travel nerves, pain, upset – a brilliant quick-fix tool) as well as using it to supplement your forgiveness practice. I'm a big fan of EFT and in cases where my clients are working on an old resentment and are experiencing physical and emotional symptoms of pain or disease, I will often combine some tapping with the forgiveness process.

Another highly recommended technique for somatic trauma release is *Somatic Experiencing* or *Trauma Healing* in the USA.

I also love the simplicity of the Hawaiian practice of forgiveness and reconciliation, *Ho'oponopono* – using the mantra "I love you, I'm sorry, Please forgive me, Thank you." The whole ritual is more complex, but the mantra can be great for emergency use. For more information start at *Wikipedia.*

On the website for *The Tools* by Phil Stutz and Barry Michels, one of the processes they share is a very short visualisation you can use in real time whilst you are having a challenging conversation - called *Active Love.* You could practice this either in advance of your Forgiveness Made Easy process, or during it.

The Sedona Method - the secret to meeting and allowing your feelings and then letting them go! Another brilliant tool for life.

PERSONAL/SPIRITUAL DEVELOPMENT ORGANISATIONS

More to Life and *More to Life US* - leading edge transformational education - in person courses and workshops.

Mindvalley - leading edge transformational education on-line and in person.

Miracle Network - resources for all things *A Course in Miracles* related - inspiration, support, magazine, events and mail order.

FORGIVENESS ORGANISATIONS

Some of the most inspiring stories of people forgiving in extreme circumstances are on YouTube — especially some of the TED talks from people who are living examples of extraordinary forgiveness. Just search 'forgiveness'.

There are also organisations such as *The Forgiveness Project* which offer resources and inspiration for forgiveness. The Forgiveness Project was founded by Marina Cantacuzino and its purpose as a secular organisation is to collect and share real-life accounts of forgiveness, to educate and inspire understanding and reflection. The project offers tools to help people reconcile with their own pain and trauma, and move on with their lives.

The *International Forgiveness Institute* - provides research and support for all aspects of forgiveness by Dr Robert Enright 'The Forgiveness Trailblazer'.

Candles Holocaust Museum and education centre was founded by Eva Kor, a Holocaust survivor, who shares her powerful story of forgiveness. A link to an inspiring interview with Eva can be found here: *https://www.youtube.com/watch?v=gdgPAetNY5U*

There are also some alternative approaches to forgiveness or processes which may serve you, for example:

Dr Fred Luskin, the director of the Stanford Forgiveness Project has a 9-step process on *Learning to Forgive.*

ON-LINE RESOURCES

I also recommend checking out the late Marshall B Rosenberg's free *Nonviolent Communication Workshop* on YouTube, because learning what he has to teach about communicating with clarity and empathy can be an enormous help to averting the build-up of future resentment in all your relationships. You can also download a crib sheet of the four pillars of *Nonviolent Communication* from his website.

The other incredible resource I recommend to any of my clients who are having relationship challenges, is the work of Alison Armstrong. Her *Queen's Code* and her website *Understand Men* offer profound, useful and amusingly delivered information about the differences between the sexes and how to be more understanding and feel more connected.

If you're interested in doing mirror work as part of your self-forgiveness process - check out Louise Hay's website or Dr Robert Holden for more information on the power of using a mirror.

BOOKS

Either I've quoted from these, or recommend them because in some way they have informed my thinking, inspired me, or are relevant to the process of letting go of the past and learning to forgive. Some are just for additional reading according to your interest.

Getting Things Done by David Allen
A Course in Miracles by Anonymous
The Queen's Code by Alison Armstrong
The Enneagram Made Easy by Renee Baron & Elizabeth Wagele
The Journey by Brandon Bays
Radical Honesty by Brad Blanton
Revolution by Russell Brand
My Stroke of Insight by Jill Bolte Taylor
Daring Greatly by Brené Brown
The Forgiveness Project by Marina Cantacuzino
Breakfast at the Victory by James P. Carse
The 7 Habits of Highly Effective People by Stephen Covey
The Wisdom of Forgiveness by the Dalai Lama and Victor Chan
Man's Search for Meaning by Viktor Frankl
The Prophet by Khalil Gibran
The Way of Mastery by Jayem/Jeshua
Loving What Is by Byron Katie
Code of the Extraordinary Mind by Vishen Lakhiani
Marrow by Elizabeth Lesser
Trauma and Memory by Peter Levine
The Honeymoon Effect by Bruce Lipton
The Biology of Belief by Bruce Lipton
Long Walk to Freedom: The Autobiography of Nelson Mandela by Nelson Mandela
Spiritual Bypassing by Robert Masters
Beyond Revenge by Michael E McCulloch
Childhood Disrupted by Donna Jackson Nakazawa
The Wisdom of Menopause by Dr Christiane Northrup
The Chimp Paradox by Dr Steve Peter

Nonviolent Communication by Marshall Rosenberg PhD

The Surrender Experiment by Michael A. Singer

The Untethered Soul by Michael A. Singer

The Tools by Phil Stutz & Barry Michels

The Power of Now by Eckhart Tolle

No Future Without Forgiveness by Desmond Tutu

Getting to Yes with Yourself by William Ury

The Integral Vision by Ken Wilber

Conscious Uncoupling by Katherine Woodward Thomas

MY RESOURCES

A FREE mp3 of me leading you step-by-step through the Forgiveness Made Easy process can be found here: *www.forgivenessmadeeasy.co.uk/bookbonus*

There's a Forgiveness Made Easy website - with links to more resources and blogs: *www.forgivenessmadeeasy.co.uk* and also a Facebook page where you can share your success stories and ask questions: *www.facebook.com/ForgivenessMadeEasy*

I also sometimes give talks on the subject of forgiveness and run live workshops. Please sign up to my mailing list to be notified of forthcoming dates: *www.forgivenessmadeeasy.co.uk/contact*

If you are a leader, you may be interested in my forthcoming on-line 9-week Advanced Leadership programme, *Leading Beyond Ego*, devised in collaboration with two evolutionary leadership colleagues, Steve Motenko and Rodney Dueck. For further details, see: *http://www.leadingbeyondego.com*

From time to time, I open up in my calendar to take on a few new one-to-one private clients or offer sessions for those who might wish to work with me personally as a VIP for a half or full day of forgiveness or evolutionary mentoring and coaching. For enquiries, please contact me through my coaching website:
www.evolutionarycoaching.co.uk

If you are a life coach or personal/spiritual development mentor and want to learn how to facilitate transformational forgiveness work with your clients, please get in touch with me through either of my websites: *www.evolutionarycoaching.co.uk* or *www.forgivenessmadeeasy.co.uk*

Whatever next steps you choose to take, I honour you and your journey towards peace in your heart and peace in our world.

"Because human nature is basically compassionate,
I believe it is possible that decades from now
we will see an era of peace –
but we must work together as global citizens of a shared planet."

His Holiness the Dalai Lama

ABOUT THE AUTHOR

Barbara J. Hunt is an author, facilitator, coach, and forgiveness specialist. She has many years' experience in transformational change and leadership training. Her private practice serves individuals and groups nationally and internationally, both on line and in person. She is also one of the core team of therapists at Vital Detox, a deliberately developmental organisation and the UK's leading health retreat specialising in emotional and physical wellbeing.

Barbara is passionate about discovering and sharing the most effective tools and practices for conscious living, working and relating and is an advocate for global peace.

Barbara is also a singer, songwriter and musician, who has released several CD albums and single tracks and has gigged throughout the UK. She currently lives in the south west of England, UK.

www.forgivenessmadeeasy.co.uk
www.evolutionarycoaching.co.uk
www.leadingbeyondego.com
www.barbarajhunt.com
www.VitalDetox.com
www.facebook.com/forgivenessmadeeasy
www.facebook.com/barbarajhuntmusician